MAKING
RESEARCH
MATTER

MAKING RESEARCH MATTER

A PSYCHOLOGIST'S GUIDE TO PUBLIC ENGAGEMENT

Edited by

LINDA R. TROPP

AMERICAN PSYCHOLOGICAL ASSOCIATION • *Washington, DC*

Published by
American Psychological Association
750 First Street, NE
Washington, DC 20002
www.apa.org

APA Order Department
P.O. Box 92984
Washington, DC 20090-2984
Tel: (800) 374-2721; Direct: (202) 336-5510
Fax: (202) 336-5502; TDD/TTY: (202) 336-6123
Online: www.apa.org/pubs/books
E-mail: order@apa.org

In the U.K., Europe, Africa, and the Middle East, copies may be ordered from
Eurospan Group
c/o Pegasus Drive
Stratton Business Park
Biggleswade Bedfordshire
SG18 8TQ United Kingdom
Phone: +44 (0) 1767 604972
Fax: +44 (0) 1767 601640
Online: https://www.eurospanbookstore.com/apa
E-mail: eurospan@turpin-distribution.com

Typeset in Minion by Circle Graphics, Inc., Columbia, MD

Printer: Sheridan Books, Chelsea, MI
Cover Designer: Naylor Design, Washington, DC

Library of Congress Cataloging-in-Publication Data

Names: Tropp, Linda R., editor.
Title: Making research matter : a psychologist's guide to public engagement / edited by Linda R. Tropp.
Description: Washington, DC : American Psychological Association, 2018. | Includes bibliographical references and index.
Identifiers: LCCN 2017019950 | ISBN 9781433828249 (paperback) | ISBN 1433828243 ()
Subjects: LCSH: Social sciences—Research. | Research—Psychological aspects. | Social participation. | BISAC: PSYCHOLOGY / Applied Psychology. | PSYCHOLOGY / Research & Methodology.
Classification: LCC H62 .M2464 2018 | DDC 300.72—dc23 LC record available at https://lccn.loc.gov/2017019950

British Library Cataloguing-in-Publication Data
A CIP record is available from the British Library.

Printed in the United States of America
First Edition

http://dx.doi.org/10.1037/0000066-000

10 9 8 7 6 5 4 3 2 1

Contents

Contributors

Max H. Bazerman, PhD, Harvard Business School, Boston, MA

Meg A. Bond, PhD, Department of Psychology, University of Massachusetts Lowell

Eugene Borgida, PhD, Department of Psychology, University of Minnesota, Minneapolis

Amanda Charbonneau, MPP, Goldman School of Public Policy, University of California, Berkeley

Abigail Dalton, MEd, Harvard Kennedy School, Cambridge, MA

John F. Dovidio, PhD, Department of Psychology, Yale University, New Haven, CT

Roberta Downing, PhD, Federal Relations, Minnesota Department of Human Services, St. Paul

Susan T. Fiske, PhD, Department of Psychology, Princeton University, Princeton, NJ

Jamie Franco-Zamudio, PhD, Department of Psychology, Spring Hill College, Mobile, AL

Jack Glaser, PhD, Goldman School of Public Policy, University of California, Berkeley

Michelle C. Haynes-Baratz, PhD, Department of Psychology, University of Massachusetts Lowell

Regina Langhout, PhD, Department of Psychology, University of California, Santa Cruz

Geoffrey Maruyama, PhD, Department of Educational Psychology, University of Minnesota, Minneapolis

Louis A. Penner, PhD, Department of Oncology, Karmanos Cancer Institute, School of Medicine, Wayne State University, Detroit, MI

Amy T. Schalet, PhD, Public Engagement Project, Department of Sociology, University of Massachusetts Amherst

Samuel R. Sommers, PhD, Department of Psychology, Tufts University, Medford, MA

Linda R. Tropp, PhD, Department of Psychological and Brain Sciences, University of Massachusetts Amherst

Lara Westerhof, PhD, Department of Educational Psychology, University of Minnesota, Minneapolis

MAKING RESEARCH MATTER

Introduction

Linda R. Tropp

Many psychology researchers have become highly effective in conveying the applied significance of academic research and serving as expert sources of scientific information. But for others of us, having such an impact might seem elusive—we might ask ourselves, "How did they do that?" while at the same time finding it hard to envision being able to do the same. Most of us have never received training in how to make our research matter or how to engage effectively with nonacademic audiences, yet these are skills we need to maximize the impact of our work.

This book is designed to fill these gaps in our professional training. Soon after I joined the faculty at the University of Massachusetts Amherst, I had the good fortune of encountering kindred spirits who share my commitment to using rigorous academic research to address social issues and serve the public interest, while enabling others to do the same. Together, we cofounded the Public Engagement Project (http://www.umass.edu/pep),

http://dx.doi.org/10.1037/0000066-001

Making Research Matter: A Psychologist's Guide to Public Engagement, L. R. Tropp (Editor)

an initiative that supports and trains faculty to engage with nonacademic audiences to inform public policy and enrich public debate. Although I began to see how many principles of effective engagement can transfer across disciplines and institutions, valuable lessons can be learned and knowledge can be gained from focusing more specifically on engagement among academic researchers in the field of psychology.

This book has therefore been developed as a resource for any psychology researcher who seeks to enhance their ability to engage with nonacademic audiences and to make their work more accessible and useful in addressing real-world concerns. The chapters in this book were written by experienced scholars who not only are excellent researchers but also have been extraordinarily effective in articulating the social relevance of their scholarship and developing productive relationships with non-academics across a broad range of institutions and public settings. Through their succinct chapters, these contributors highlight key insights gained from years of experience and provide readers with tips and strategies that can facilitate their engaged work. As a whole, this book will help psychology researchers—and potentially researchers in other social science disciplines—to develop greater confidence and skill in communicating and working with nonacademics, while enabling those with prior engagement experience to broaden the domains in which they work.

As we consider embarking on a path to engagement, it can be useful to reflect on the many different ways in which we might become an engaged scholar. Perhaps the first image that comes to mind is the prospect of seeing our name or that of a colleague in the media. Clearly, this can be an effective way to broaden the reach of our work, and we can adopt a variety of specific strategies to share our work effectively through such means. Chapter 2 by Schalet and Chapter 3 by Sommers focus on these strategies to prepare readers for writing op-ed pieces and blog entries for high-profile news outlets, being interviewed for radio or television, or publishing a book for a popular audience.

But there are also many other models for engagement and approaches we can take toward becoming an engaged scholar. Depending on our goals and interests, we might want our research to inform public policy at the local, state, or national levels; in particular, Chapter 4 by Downing and Chapter 5 by Dalton and Bazerman describe how to approach and work with policymakers and government agencies to have maximum impact. Instead, we might seek to engage with the legal system or law enforcement. In Chapter 6, Borgida and Fiske provide crucial insights regarding how scientific evidence can be used in litigation, and in Chapter 7 Glaser and Charbonneau detail strategies for establishing effective collaborations with law enforcement. Alternatively, we may seek greater involvement working within social institutions and communities; Maruyama and Westerhof (Chapter 8), Penner (Chapter 9), and Bond and Haynes-Baratz (Chapter 10) offer both specific guidelines and broad insights regarding how best to cultivate partnerships within schools, hospitals, and community-based organizations. We might also seek guidance about how to train students to work effectively in these settings and how varied forms of engagement can mesh with our other professional goals, issues addressed by Franco-Zamudio and Langhout (Chapter 11) and Dovidio (Chapter 12). Whatever forms of engagement match who you are and what you care about, this book aims to provide you with crucial insights and knowledge that will enhance your ability to make your research matter.[1]

---

[1] The chapters included in this book focus heavily on engagement activities in public domains and social institutions as they often emerge in the United States. Admittedly and regrettably, this single edited volume cannot do justice to the vast and dynamic ways in which relations with public audiences and social institutions are likely to vary around the world. But it is my hope that psychology researchers from other countries will find insights that are useful and relevant to their own societies' social, political, and institutional contexts.

1

Becoming an Engaged Scholar: Getting Started

Linda R. Tropp

The research needed for social practice . . . is a type of action research,
a comparative research of the conditions and effects of various forms
of social action, and research leading to social action. Research
that produces nothing but books will not suffice.

—Kurt Lewin (1946)

Many of us start off our academic careers with a vague hope that the work we do will somehow, someday contribute to making the world a better place. As a graduate student, I remember reading through the curriculum vitae of one of my mentors, Thomas Pettigrew, who in the 1960s served as a member of the White House Task Force on Education and as a consultant to the U.S. Commission on Civil Rights (Cherry, 2008). At the time, I remember doubting that it would ever be possible for a young researcher like me to have such an ability or opportunity to

http://dx.doi.org/10.1037/0000066-002
Making Research Matter: A Psychologist's Guide to Public Engagement, L. R. Tropp (Editor)

contribute to the public good and feeling wistful for that golden age when social psychological research seemed to have greater real-world impact—harkening back to the oft-cited social science statement presented in the 1954 *Brown v. Board of Education* case, which helped to persuade the U.S. Supreme Court of the need to desegregate our public schools (see Chapter 12, this volume).

The truth is, many of us are driven by a desire to lend our scientific expertise to pressing social issues, current events, and public debates. And many of us have asked ourselves questions such as "How do I get started in doing this kind of work?" without necessarily knowing where to look for the answer. My hope is that this chapter will help to get you started on your own path toward engaged scholarship. On the basis of my own experiences over the past 20 years—spanning from my time in graduate school to my current life as a professor—I propose that your path begins with asking yourself a series of related questions regarding the kind of impact you most wish to have and the kinds of activities, roles, and goals that are most important and of interest to you.

WHAT ISSUE DO I CARE MOST ABOUT?

One of the first things I would encourage you to do is to think about the social issue that you care most about. In other words, if your research could help to effect one change in the world, what would it be? Improving the quality of public education? Reducing racial disparities in health care? Enhancing workers' resilience to stress? Here, the more precise you can be, the better—for example, if you care about improving the quality of public education, what aspects of this issue are you most passionate about? Teacher training? Curriculum reform? Bullying and violence in schools? Encouraging interest in science among girls and young women? Numerous issues could benefit greatly from your input and expertise, and an integral part of engagement is figuring out the issue (or issues) for which you are most willing to invest your time and energy.

Also, note that once you become engaged in work with nonacademic audiences, you begin to develop a track record and become known for doing this kind of work. Before too long, you will probably find yourself crossing paths with other individuals and organizations who are committed to the same issues, which can swiftly lead to many additional opportunities for engagement around these issues in the future. So, it's probably worthwhile for you to take some time to think of what you care most about to build a foundation for engagement activities that will allow you to forge new relationships and sustain your involvement over time.

WHAT KINDS OF ACTIVITIES INTEREST ME MOST?

Next, take a moment to consider the kinds of activities that interest you the most, the skills you have to offer, and the ways in which you work best. For example, do you prefer being in the spotlight or working behind the scenes? Speaking off-the-cuff or preparing remarks in advance? Working independently or in dialogue with others? Focusing on concrete goals in the short term or envisioning broader goals over the long term? Although such practical considerations are sometimes overlooked, answers to any and all of these questions can help guide us toward making contributions that we find fulfilling and that play to our strengths, thereby enhancing the likelihood that we'll want to stay engaged over time.

This is not to say that we shouldn't also attempt to develop new skills as we try new things or that we'll know right away the activities for which we are best suited. As with many things, a process of trial and error may be involved, but through experience, we can gain a better sense of the activities we find to be most compelling and for which we are particularly well-suited, as well as those for which we seek to develop greater skill. Personally, I have tended to gravitate toward engagement activities that involve what I would consider more behind-the-scenes work, translating scientific research for policy, legal, and nongovernmental organizations—what I have often thought of as the academic's equivalent to being a law clerk for a judge or a pollster for a political campaign. I have felt more comfortable identifying the organization's needs and distilling research in ways that are relevant for their goals than being in the spotlight, such as by delivering expert testimony in a courtroom or getting into the fray of public debates. Nonetheless, several years ago, the Public Engagement Project at the University of Massachusetts Amherst sponsored an op-ed writing workshop, and I was curious enough to try my hand at writing in this format. As I noticed my colleagues gleefully diving into honing their arguments through eloquent prose, I remember feeling trapped—indeed, to me, it felt like the class went on forever and it couldn't end soon enough, though a colleague recently reminded me that it was only a half-day workshop!

It soon became clear to me that writing an op-ed does not fit my skill set, nor does it feel like the kind of contribution I'm supposed to make; more generally, I am more inclined to pursue engagement activities that involve conversation and mutual exchange, rather than those that involve argumentation or stating a case. Learning this about myself has opened me up to a range of engagement activities that feel much more natural to me—and that are just as capable of having a meaningful real-world impact as those that may be more in the spotlight. For instance, I have served as an expert reviewer for amicus briefs submitted to the U.S. Supreme Court for cases concerning the use of race in university admissions (e.g., *Fisher v. University of Texas*, 2016) and school assignment within public school districts (e.g., *Parents Involved in Community Schools v. Seattle School District*, 2007); in this role, I seek to provide litigators and policy advocates with compelling social science evidence relevant to each case while also ensuring that any academic research cited is presented accurately to the court (see Chapter 6, this volume). I have also been invited to present at congressional briefings on prejudice, discriminatory profiling, and immigration and to deliver workshops on racial bias to educators, public defenders, and nongovernmental organizations, with the goal of making academic research on these topics as accessible as possible and directly relevant to informing the work they do (see Chapters 4, 7, and 8). What I especially enjoy about these kinds of engagement activities is the opportunity to learn about the goals of varied groups involved in social justice work, which then allows me to tailor presentations of scientific knowledge in direct relation to their goals and to engage in back-and-forth discussions about how the research we conduct can help them to achieve their goals (Schalet, Tropp, & Troy, 2017).

Moreover, from these kinds of engagement activities, I have gained deeper insights into the issues at play and how legislators, litigators, policy advocates, and educators are likely to think about them; in turn, these insights enhance my ability to speak to the value of scientific research when I participate in other forms of engagement, such as granting media interviews or writing for popular outlets.

Please keep in mind that the examples I provide above merely represent some of my own experiences in the world of engaged scholarship, and the kinds of engagement activities I have described may not suit everyone. I raise these examples simply to illustrate the wide variety of engagement activities in which any of us might become involved. Ultimately, though, I believe it is up to each of us to explore our own interests and determine the kinds of contributions to engaged scholarship that we feel most compelled to pursue.

WHO COULD BENEFIT MOST FROM THE EXPERTISE I HAVE TO OFFER?

Once you have some clarity regarding the issue(s) you care most about and the kinds of activities that interest you, then you can begin to think about the audiences who could benefit the most from your scholarly expertise. Ask yourself: Who needs to know what I know? Keep in mind that answering this question will likely involve some additional research on your part. For example, you might conduct internet searches of organizations involved with the issue, ranging from civic organizations at the local level to policy organizations on the national stage to nongovernmental organizations working internationally. Or perhaps you might find a quote in the newspaper by a community leader or state official about the very issue you care about, or you might come across a report from a government agency or policy advocate, and you can easily envision adding to the conversation they've already begun. In my experience with a variety of organizations, people are usually pretty happy to hear from someone with scholarly expertise who can usefully add to the work they are already doing.

HOW WELL DO I KNOW THEM AND THEIR GOALS?

But before you pick up the phone or send an e-mail, take stock of how well you do (or don't) understand the goals and needs of the person or organization whom you wish to contact. How confident are you that you understand what these individuals, institutions, or communities need, from their perspective? How much do you know about how they work, what constraints or timelines they are working under, the terminology they use, or how they might frame the issue you care about in similar or different ways? I believe one of the common pitfalls we academics face in our attempts to communicate our work to nonacademic audiences is our tendency to underestimate how much translation is actually necessary. A large part of this effort involves changing how we talk about our research and why it matters (Badgett, 2016). Understandably, given our disciplinary training, we are likely to have grown accustomed to talking about the value of our research in terms of what people in our discipline want to know—for example, how the research extends our understanding of some aspect of human functioning, cognition, motivation, or behavior. Instead, when describing our work to nonacademic audiences or community partners, we need to explain why the research matters for their specific goals and how the research might help them to achieve these goals—for example, getting a piece of legislation passed, winning a court case, publishing a front-page story, implementing a policy, or changing an institutional practice. Thus, the more knowledgeable we are about others' goals and needs, the more effective and impactful we can be in translating the expertise we have.

AM I REALLY READY TO GET INVOLVED?

Still, even if we've done our homework and learned as much as we can about others' goals and needs, we might be a bit cautious about plunging into the world of engagement. Perhaps this is in part because we wonder whether we—as individual researchers or as a research community— really know enough about the topic at hand or whether we have amassed sufficient scientific evidence to warrant sharing this information widely with the goal of having broader impact. As researchers, we tend to feel more comfortable speaking in terms of generalities and probabilities than in terms of specifics and absolutes; as such, it might feel unnerving to think that a journalist might publicize our research without revealing its nuances or that a policymaker or community organization might choose a particular course of action based on our or others' research findings (Eagly, 2016; see also Chapter 2, this volume).

Here, I think it can be useful for us to remember that we don't necessarily need to have all the answers and that the level of knowledge and expertise we do have can still be quite useful. Indeed, I recall once being contacted by a newspaper reporter who asked me about a topic that, from my perspective, fell somewhat beyond my central areas of expertise. He was writing about an underdog sports team that was making a great comeback, and he wanted to focus this Cinderella story around the following question: What is it about humans that makes us embrace winners? (Davis, 2008). Given that most of my academic work has focused on intergroup processes and I know virtually nothing about sports, I hesitated to comment and offered suggestions for other people whom he could contact. Yet he was quick to remind me of all the people in the world who are more than happy to respond to journalists' questions and be quoted in the media without having any scientific background or expertise whatsoever. And to him, my PhD degree meant—as he later noted in the article—that I have "more pedigrees than a rich woman's dog." This experience and several others have reminded me how, even if we might not have all the answers, the information and expertise we do have is still of value. As long as we are honest in sharing our expertise while maintaining our scientific integrity, we can simply explain what we know or don't know, including where gaps exist between existing knowledge in the research literature and the answers or information others might want. And, as with just about any skill, we often become more adept at sharing our expertise and communicating scientific information with greater experience and practice.

IS IT WORTH IT TO GET INVOLVED?

In addition, if we're really honest with ourselves, it could be that some of our reservations about engaged scholarship stem from questions regarding whether it is worth all the effort. Particularly if we feel like our schedules are already quite full, concerns about the time and energy we might devote to engaged scholarship could loom large. I think it's worthwhile for us to pay attention to these concerns and set realistic expectations for ourselves, keeping in mind that our professional lives can have many chapters as our work schedules ebb and flow. In this context, you might find it useful to reflect on questions such as the following: Is this really the right time for me to become more engaged in work outside of academia? Do I have too much on my plate right now? What trade-offs would I need to make to become more engaged? Would more engaged scholarship pull me away from other obligations and goals that are priorities for me? At the same time as we consider factors that might limit our engagement, we should also remember to pay attention to the multitude of factors that might drive us to become more engaged. Recognizing that academic scholarship and engagement activities can often complement each other (see Chapter 12, this volume), we might think about the ways in which engagement can enhance our research, teaching, or professional training or how it might create a foundation for our future academic and professional goals. We might also think about how opportunities for engagement might give us, and our research, a greater sense of purpose or meaning.

As a personal example, as an assistant professor I was asked to present at a public forum in relation to a court case concerning a school district's plan to achieve benefits of racial diversity in public schools (*Comfort v. Lynn School Committee*, 2004); afterward, the organizer invited me to join a statewide initiative focused on reducing hate crimes, harassment, and discrimination in public schools sponsored by the Commonwealth of Massachusetts Attorney General's Office. On a professional level, I felt strongly that getting involved in this initiative would give me valuable insights into how scientific theories and research evidence could be used to promote racial integration in schools; perhaps even more fundamentally, on a personal level, much of why I do what I do as an academic has been driven by a desire to reduce the harms posed by racial prejudice and discrimination and to promote positive interracial relations, particularly among youth. At the same time, running through the back of my head was the not-so-subtle message I received from some professional colleagues suggesting that "it's nice that you do these things, but they're not going to get you tenure." Ultimately, after weighing numerous pros and cons, I decided that this engagement opportunity was important enough to me to pursue, for both personal and professional reasons; but it was still critical for me to realistically consider the potential benefits and costs of becoming engaged before making this decision.

WHAT KIND OF RELATIONSHIP DO I WISH TO HAVE WITH THOSE I WANT TO REACH?

If and when you do decide to become an engaged scholar, other issues to consider involve the kind of relationship you wish to have and the type of role you wish to play with the nonacademic audiences you seek to reach (Fischhoff, 2013; Pettigrew, 1967; Pielke, 2007). Many academic researchers see engagement primarily in terms of disseminating scientific knowledge to individuals and organizations who might benefit from this work. But academic researchers can also choose whether, and to what degree, they might become more directly involved in helping these entities to achieve their goals. For example, some researchers may want to work more closely with individuals and organizations by using their knowledge and expertise to help them evaluate strengths and weaknesses of a variety of policy options, to assist in the implementation of certain programs, or to advocate for specific positions or decisions in light of the scientific evidence. Regardless of the kinds of relationships we decide to cultivate, we should make efforts to communicate our views about what we can or cannot do, or what we are willing or not willing to do, with our nonacademic partners and collaborators. Having open discussions about the nature and depth of our potential involvement is crucial to establish a shared understanding and to minimize confusion or frustration—both for ourselves and for our prospective partners.

More generally, it can be useful for academic researchers to invest time in getting to know and learn about the mission and goals of nonacademic collaborators to assess whether they are compatible as partners before becoming overly committed to or involved in their work. This might be accomplished through having a series of exploratory discussions before embarking on a project or perhaps working on a small project together before launching a larger initiative. Such approaches can help us to determine the extent to which our goals are aligned, how we each frame the relevant issues, and whether we envision similar or different strategies and courses of action to achieve our respective goals. If through this process you determine that your goals are aligned and compatible, then these initial discussions and projects can lay the groundwork for a more productive, long-term collaboration, and if not, then you can more easily extricate yourself from what could potentially become an unsatisfactory work relationship.

Sometimes points of divergence between academic researchers and nonacademic collaborators involve the degree to which we seek to focus on universal principles versus specific contexts in our work. Academic researchers in psychology have traditionally sought to identify general principles that guide human cognition, emotion, motivation, and behavior across situations and contexts, whereas nonacademics are typically more concerned with the question of what works to address problems in a specific situation or context. Nonetheless, many academics have highlighted the need to attend to both universalities in human experience and the ways in which psychological processes manifest themselves differently across social, cultural, and historical contexts (Bronfenbrenner, 1979; Norenzayan & Heine, 2005; Pettigrew, 1991). Adopting a contextualized approach can often help to bridge gaps between scientific research and its practical application because greater contextualization establishes crucial links between abstract theoretical principles and the concrete social realities relevant to policy and intervention (see, e.g., Brewer, 1997; Killen, Rutland, & Ruck, 2011; Stephan, 2006).

Additional points of divergence might involve how we see the role of values in science and whether, or to what degree, we believe academic research should be held independent from its potential applied value. Academic researchers are often encouraged to maintain a separation between their personal values and scientific pursuits for fear that their values could interfere with an ability to remain objective in conducting research and interpreting research findings. Yet we academics also care deeply about the issues we study, and we often choose to pursue research programs precisely because they are linked to our values, with the hopes of enhancing people's lives and contributing to the public good. Like others (Crosby, Clayton, Downing, & Iyer, 2004; Eagly, 2016; Schalet et al., 2017), I believe it is possible to pursue engaged scholarship in accordance with our values, without necessarily compromising our scientific integrity or research rigor. Yet I also believe that each individual researcher must assess for themselves what stance to take regarding the role of values in their scientific pursuits and what kinds of engaged relationships make the most sense for their own academic career and trajectory.

HOW CAN ENGAGEMENT FIT WITH THE REST OF MY ACADEMIC LIFE?

At the same time as we contemplate these issues, it is worth taking a serious look at how we see engagement activities meshing with our other professional goals (see Chapter 12, this volume). Keep in mind that engaged scholarship can often be quite time-consuming. This is especially likely to be the case for those who seek to develop long-term partnerships with social institutions and community-based organizations, as it takes considerable time and effort to build the kinds of trusting and productive relationships that foster the greatest potential for success (see, e.g., Chapter 10, this volume).

But even when we have more modest goals, we would do well to remain mindful of how much time and energy we commit to engagement around social issues in relation to the other professional goals we set out to achieve. As with so many other aspects of our academic lives, we need to recognize that our time and energy are limited (and precious) resources, and we should budget those resources accordingly. It is understandable that when we are just starting to become engaged scholars, we are especially eager to make a difference and to take advantage of opportunities that come our way. It can also be exciting and gratifying for us to experience interest in our scholarship among those who are particularly well-suited to apply it in practice. Oftentimes, through sharing our expertise, we can inject new energy into the activities of the organizations with which we work. But at some point, we might also need to be strategic or selective regarding our involvement. Once real-world organizations know that we exist, that we have useful information to share, and that we share a commitment to the same issues, we might be invited to participate in a multitude of projects and initiatives, such that we run the risk of getting pulled in too many directions and spreading ourselves too thin. It can be useful, then, to periodically take a step back and reflect on how engagement fits within the broader constellation of our professional goals, so that we can feel good about the engagement activities we decide to take on and feel more prepared to sustain our commitment to engaged scholarship over time.

CONCLUDING THOUGHTS

Being an engaged scholar can be exciting and invigorating, and it can often give deeper meaning to the academic work we do. Collectively, as a discipline, we have only begun to cultivate the presence and influence we could potentially have in the public sphere, speaking to the broader relevance of psychological research for people's lives and society at large. Growing numbers of academic psychologists now actively maintain a dual commitment to scientific work and meaningful engagement outside of academia, in line with Lewin's (1946) original call for action research. Many scholars have embraced the challenges of forging partnerships with nongovernmental, community, and policy organizations, at the same time as greater value is being granted to socially relevant research within the mainstream of our field. As such, I believe the time is ripe for academic psychologists to renew our commitment to conducting rigorous scientific research and identifying ways to put this research to good use. May this chapter, and the chapters that follow, help you to do just that.

REFERENCES

Badgett, M. V. L. (2016). *The public professor: How to use your research to change the world*. New York, NY: New York University Press.

Brewer, M. (1997). The social psychology of intergroup relations: Can research inform practice? *Journal of Social Issues, 53*, 197–211. http://dx.doi.org/10.1111/j.1540-4560.1997.tb02440.x

Bronfenbrenner, U. (1979). *The ecology of human development*. Cambridge, MA: Harvard University Press.

Brown v. Board of Education, 347 U.S. 483 (1954).

Cherry, F. (2008). Thomas F. Pettigrew: Building on the scholar-activist tradition in social psychology. In U. Wagner, L. R. Tropp, G. Finchilescu, & C. G. Tredoux (Eds.), *Improving intergroup relations: Building on the legacy of Thomas F. Pettigrew* (pp. 11–23). http://dx.doi.org/10.1002/9781444303117.ch2

Comfort v. Lynn School Committee, 418 F.3d (2004).

Crosby, F. J., Clayton, S., Downing, R. A., & Iyer, A. (2004). Values and science. *American Psychologist, 59,* 125–126. http://dx.doi.org/10.1037/0003-066X.59.2.125

Davis, M. (2008, May 2). City embraces Cinderella Hawks. *Atlanta Journal-Constitution,* p. A1.

Eagly, A. H. (2016). When passionate advocates meet research on diversity, does the honest broker stand a chance? *Journal of Social Issues, 72,* 199–222. http://dx.doi.org/10.1111/josi.12163

Fischhoff, B. (2013). The sciences of science communication. *Proceedings of the National Academy of Sciences of the United States of America, 110*(Suppl. 3), 14033–14039. http://dx.doi.org/10.1073/pnas.1213273110

Fisher v. University of Texas, 579 U.S. ____ (2016).

Killen, M., Rutland, A., & Ruck, M. (2011). Promoting equity, tolerance, and justice in childhood: Policy implications. *Policy Report: Sharing Child and Youth Development Knowledge, 25,* 1–33.

Lewin, K. (1946). Action research and minority problems. *Journal of Social Issues, 2,* 34–46. http://dx.doi.org/10.1111/j.1540-4560.1946.tb02295.x

Norenzayan, A., & Heine, S. J. (2005). Psychological universals: What are they and how can we know? *Psychological Bulletin, 131,* 763–784. http://dx.doi.org/10.1037/0033-2909.131.5.763

Parents Involved in Community Schools v. Seattle School District, 551 U.S. 701 (2007).

Pettigrew, T. F. (1967, Fall). SPSSI as honest broker. *Society for the Psychological Study of Social Issues Newsletter,* 117.

Pettigrew, T. F. (1991). Toward unity and bold theory: Popperian suggestions for two persistent problems of social psychology. In C. W. Stephan, W. G. Stephan, & T. Pettigrew (Eds.), *The future of social psychology: Defining the relationship between sociology and psychology* (pp. 13–27). http://dx.doi.org/10.1007/978-1-4612-3120-2_2

Pielke, R. A. (2007). *The honest broker: Making sense of science in policy and politics.* http://dx.doi.org/10.1017/CBO9780511818110

Schalet, A. T., Tropp, L. R., & Troy, L. M. (2017). *A relational model of public engagement: Making research usable.* Manuscript in preparation.

Stephan, W. G. (2006). Bridging the researcher-practitioner divide in intergroup relations. *Journal of Social Issues, 62,* 597–605. http://dx.doi.org/10.1111/j.1540-4560.2006.00475.x

2

The Media: Helping Journalists Use and Interpret Your Research

Amy T. Schalet

*I am looking for something I can only call companionship: other people
who are, like me, trying to understand what the hell is going on here,
in the society or societies we find ourselves embedded in.*

—Barbara Ehrenreich (2007), journalist and *New York Times* best-selling author

"Companionship" is not the word that comes to mind when most researchers imagine interfacing with members of the media. Yet, journalist and former *New York Times* columnist Barbara Ehrenreich's (2007) word choice in her "Journalist's Plea" articulates exactly how I have felt about dozens of exchanges with reporters. These encounters with journalists left me feeling invigorated, curious about new questions, and gratified to have spent time thinking together with another human being about things I care deeply about. Invariably, I would have liked to change small, nonessential details afterward. But nine times out of 10, I have enjoyed

http://dx.doi.org/10.1037/0000066-003
Making Research Matter: A Psychologist's Guide to Public Engagement, L. R. Tropp (Editor)

and benefited from the story that resulted—for instance, by garnering wider readership of my scholarship and further opportunities for public engagement.

Like many academics, I have established my reputation through research that I published in peer-reviewed venues, primarily in journal articles and in a university-press book. And like most academics, I assumed, all along, that the knowledge I labored hard to produce would somehow filter down to other members of society who could use it. However, toward the end of graduate school, it dawned on me that such filtering down was not guaranteed (Schalet, 2016). Luckily, I happened upon opportunities to interface with professionals and media specialists, and I started doing presentations for health practitioners and researchers. Over time, those presentations, coupled with interviews with print media and radio reporters, one high-stakes TV interview, and half a dozen opinion editorials and general audience articles, have enabled me to share my research with parents, educators, providers, policymakers, and shapers of our culture. There have been many benefits to going down this road: a greater sense of purpose and satisfaction with my profession; new perspective on my area of expertise; current, often unpublished policy and public health developments; new research questions; and potential opportunities for research funding.

But the path has not been straightforward. Few of the skills and networks I needed to accomplish these forms of engagement were part of my disciplinary socialization. Even after gaining such skills through unanticipated opportunities as a postdoctoral fellow, I have found that intensive media engagement is met with ambivalence in the academic community. Much as it welcomes positive attention, the university does not have an incentive structure to reward excellence in media dissemination, and getting research into the media, and doing it right, takes time and is not accounted for in typical measures of faculty productivity. Sometimes peers look admiringly at us, but sometimes they look askance and question the seriousness of our scholarly commitments. Still, the work is more than worth it. We owe it to taxpayers who foot the bill for our grant dollars. We owe it to our democracy to help inform public dialogue. And along the way, some of us will be fortunate to find like-minded academic colleagues who are willing to support each other in engaged scholarship, such as those with whom I cofounded the Public Engagement Project at the University of Massachusetts Amherst, which I currently direct (see the introduction to this volume and https://www.umass.edu/pep/guides-resources).

In this chapter, I draw on our challenges and victories to detail the lessons that I have learned about conceptualizing media encounters, the rules of the game, the importance of preparation and improvisation, and dealing with tricky issues. I believe these lessons are relevant to social and behavioral scientists from many disciplines—indeed, to scientists across the board.

WHAT IS IT THAT WE'RE DOING WHEN WE ENGAGE THE MEDIA?

Although many of us admire famous public intellectuals, when it comes to doing this work ourselves, researchers are often wary of entering the fray. One reason is that we're often a bit suspicious of the motivations of the parties involved: researchers who self-promote and betray their craft by oversimplifying, journalists who misquote or distort by taking words out of context, and editors who cut crucial information or lead with faulty titles. Rather than be guided by the specter of mutual misunderstanding and misuse of information, we might envision exchanges with journalists and editors as, ideally, mutually enriching dialogues. Not only do these dialogues give us the opportunity to share knowledge with audiences beyond the academy, they also give us the opportunity to learn about new angles on our topic. We might think of preparing for these exchanges as akin to preparing for conference presentations. Just as we have all had to learn the rules of the game to create gratifying conference presentations—getting the format, length, and content right—creating a satisfying encounter with the popular media requires an understanding of its structure. As we start out, we mostly play by the rules of its game, but once we've mastered the rules, we can also improvise and really have fun with it.

RULE 1 OF THE GAME: NO TIME LIKE THE PRESENT

Although the best of scholarship and journalism have much in common—curiosity, willingness to ask hard questions, and craftsmanship in using language to answer those questions—the practitioners of each craft work in different universes. Learning to successfully bridge the cultures of these professions requires the ability to manage those differences, which I believe center on two rules of the game. The first one pertains to time. Borrowing again from Barbara Ehrenreich as she characterizes journalism and sociology, I would like to share a sentence that I believe pertains to scholarship more generally: "If there is a single crucial difference, it is in the two professions' relationship to time" (p. 231). Indeed, a scholar "can burrow in her office for years with a single project; a journalist usually has hours, days, or at best a few weeks in which to absorb a body of material and fashion it into a sharply pointed, communicable form" (Ehrenreich, 2007, pp. 231–232). Ehrenreich's words will not come as a surprise to researchers who have interfaced with media. We know the seemingly unreasonable time demands from journalists who contact us with questions and requests for responses within days, sometimes within hours.

But it is worth considering for a moment the perspective of a journalist on this time bind: She can never, wrote Ehrenreich (citing Walter Benjamin) "step out of the 'storm'" of rapidly changing news. Eager to get it right and to acknowledge the complexity of the matter, but with extremely limited time to do that, journalists such as Ehrenreich approach scholars with a kind of hopeful neediness, as if to say, "You, we figure, have had the time to comb through the data and reflect on the results." Although they have some tried-and-true colleagues in academia, journalists often have no way to know who the real experts are. Even when they do, their calls often go unanswered. Ehrenreich recalled the spring of 2014, when Bill Cosby was spouting tirades against poor African Americans. She was desperate to locate a researcher to demonstrate what she correctly suspected was the erroneous nature of Cosby's accusations. Ehrenreich did locate such a researcher, who responded quickly—and with journalistic gold: a "succinct 'expert' quote." Yet, she could not help but be disappointed: Why was this expert not proactive? When she asked him to write an op-ed and offered to help place it, he demurred: "He was too busy, maybe in a few weeks. Well, in a few weeks it might be too late. Cosby's accusations would have blown through the collective consciousness without refutation" (Ehrenreich, 2007, pp. 232–233).

The unrealized potential of researchers to contribute to the common good and drive important decisions is nothing short of a tragedy—and the misinformation run amok, a travesty. But the only way to confront the time bind in which journalists and academics find themselves is to understand and respect both. We cannot, nor should we, change the essential differences between academic and journalistic time: as researchers, our methodical, plodding, deliberative nature—which leads to our slowness—is our great strength. At the same time, we can keep the slowness with which we—as a general rule of thumb—deliver our results from getting in our way of efforts to get our research into the media. Here I offer three strategies to honor the journalist's relationship to time while staying true to ours. In the immediate term: Respond and, if necessary, refer out; in the interim: prepare and practice; in the longer term: hook and rehook.

Respond Immediately

I suggest responding swiftly to journalists, even if we do not know whether we want to or can help them. A quick e-mail to recognize receipt and to ask for clarification on the request—what is the journalist's time line, what is the angle on the story, what is the journalist ideally looking for—will meet a ground rule for potential companionship and do so without making any commitment. A quick response, regardless of what one can offer, is particularly important for journalists who must make immediate decisions about whether to keep looking for an expert. An initial e-mail response will give them information with which to make those next decisions. But it also can benefit you: You win time to decide what to do. You can also solicit information that can help you make your decision, and if need be, you (or perhaps your university news office) can do a quick background check on the legitimacy of the reporter and news outlet in question. By responding quickly to that first e-mail a reporter sends, we are able to establish the basis for a relationship that can lead to better media opportunities later on—even when we say "no, not now" or "no, not me" in the present. Sometimes we can do something else that costs us little but is very valuable for the reporter: Refer to another expert or give factual information over e-mail without having to go on record.

To illustrate, I was recently contacted by a reporter to explain a trend in adolescent sexual health. In his interview request, the reporter led me to suspect that his operating assumptions were inaccurate, and his assumptions had the potential to misinform policymaking. Someone had to set him straight, but I did not have the time or published facts to do so in print. I referred the reporter to a research institute I knew had the expertise to communicate carefully about a politically contentious issue. Meanwhile, I shared with him—off the record—my best understanding of the current status of knowledge on the issue. He expressed gratitude for the referral and for my correction, assuring me he would not quote me. Similarly, I was asked recently by a reputable national TV station to comment on a particularly controversial issue. The producer was persuasive and almost convinced me to say yes, in spite of my gut feeling that I neither knew the necessary literature to comment wisely nor had the time to bone up on it. After mulling it over for 2 days, I said no. My university news office was disappointed, but the producer respected my decision. She even promised to be back in touch in the future for a segment on adolescent sexuality that was right in my wheelhouse. There are times to go out on a media limb, and I have done so. But neither of these opportunities was a limb on which I wanted to go. By responding swiftly, considering the request, and referring to colleagues when I said no, I showed goodwill and built relationships that had the potential to generate future opportunities.

Prepare and Practice

It is essential to prepare and practice before going on record. As many a scholar seeking to reach nonacademic audiences will attest, the effort we put into mastering public communications will return its value in kind, first and foremost by forcing us to clarify our thinking. In a recent article in *The Conversation*, psychologists Jonathan Wai and David Miller (2015) wrote, "Not only did the process [of writing for the public] improve the quality of our writing, but it also brought more clarity to the way we were thinking about scientific problems." At the Public Engagement Project, I have seen our faculty fellows have similar experiences in their media message trainings and even in their conversations with their peers across different disciplines. These experiences forced them to become much clearer than they were at the start about what exactly they were thinking.

One way to gain clarity in your thinking, while relating your thoughts to current events, is to practice through the format of op-ed writing. Who has not at some point thought, "My research could really inform that important news story; I'd write an op-ed if those recommendations, lectures, and meetings weren't already filling up my week"? Then once we manage to sit down to draft the op-ed, we find the news cycle has long moved on. Here the problem runs deeper than the difference between academic and journalistic timetables. For in addition to scheduling and squeamishness, one reason that many of us can't whip up that op-ed when the news needs us is that we simply do not know how to. We may write for a living, but engaging, complicating, and persuading in 900 words is an art unto its own, and one that requires a great deal of practice. If you practice this art well in advance of the moment you might need to act quickly, you have the chance to gain the mastery—and ideally some paragraphs of rough drafts—that make it possible to jump on opportunities that the news cycle may present.

What are the features of the op-ed format? The building blocks are short, active-tense sentences, and—this is essential—paragraphs of one to three (definitely no more than five) sentences. You cannot make your point using theory or method. The point must speak to people's real lives. By the end of the fifth sentence, readers need to see a main argument clearly stated or evocatively foreshadowed. That argument cannot be solely analytic, such as a short version of an academic analysis explaining a puzzle or a historical contextualization of a modern-day phenomenon. It must contain—explicitly or implicitly—a normative perspective, that is, an argument about what should happen. As researchers, we ground that argument in our best understanding of the evidence, but in the op-ed format, we cannot rely on data to speak for themselves; we must clarify their implications. Lead with concrete examples—stories, metaphors, anecdotes, compelling statistics—and precede any analysis and concepts with such concrete examples. Where relevant, speak personally, evoking your experience, emotion, passion, and conviction. And the closing is key: Always conclude with a strong, unequivocal synthetic statement, driving it home with humor, a sense of heft, or, ideally, both.

Hook and Rehook Your Message

Practicing op-ed writing gives you the opportunity to develop your main media messages, which will stand you in good stead in other kinds of media engagement. But once you're ready, how do you get media attention for your research story? Sometimes, if we're lucky and have a good publicity team (through a university, a journal or press, or other professional public relations assistance), our research *is* the news. But generally, the trick is to hook our research stories on current events as they emerge both unexpectedly and predictably—in the case of yearly anniversaries, holidays, or the back-to-school season, for example. If we have practiced the format of op-ed writing in advance, then we can be in the position to, with little notice, hook or wrap a stored-away draft around a current event. Rehooking can happen even after the moment has past. My first op-ed came into print that way. After I practiced the format of op-ed writing in workshop in the spring of 2008, the perfect hook for my research on adolescent sexuality presented itself on Labor Day weekend of the same year: News hit that the party that endorsed so-called abstinence-only education had nominated a vice presidential candidate whose 17-year-old daughter had been just reported to be pregnant. I seized the moment and sure enough, within days a national newspaper accepted my op-ed draft.

But just as we were finalizing details for publication, Lehman Brothers announced its bankruptcy. Sarah Palin's daughter was no longer news, and publication of my op-ed was delayed week after week. I had already decided my moment had come and gone when in early October, after a cringe-worthy vice presidential debate, a colleague suggested I rehook my op-ed around the question about why sex education was missing from the debate. I went home, rewrote the first paragraph, and sent an e-mail to the newspaper editor suggesting the new hook. A few days later, *The Washington Post* printed "A Question for Sarah Palin." The truth is that most problems, whether we're talking about sex education, racial stereotypes, or climate change, as well as the demand for our expertise, are not transient. Chances are that if the expert whom Ehrenreich consulted did write that op-ed after a few weeks, he would not have been able to place it then. But he would have drafted facts and arguments in a piece he could have quickly rehooked on current events in the future.

RULE 2 OF THE GAME: TELL A STORY

If the first rule of the game pertains to understanding and finding ways to reconcile—if not perfectly synchronize—the academic and journalistic relationship to time, the second rule of the game pertains to mastering the format in which to communicate knowledge journalists can use. What format makes our knowledge usable to reporters? Leading science communication specialist Nancy Baron answered that question succinctly in her 2010 book titled *Escape From the Ivory Tower: A Guide to Making Your Science Matter*. "Tell Me a Story: What Journalists Want From You" is the title of the chapter instructing researchers on how to overcome the typical clash of cultures between academia and journalism. Similar calls have come from publicly engaged scholars within the academy. Psychologist Steven Pinker (2014) urged scholars to abandon the often unnecessary contortions of conventional academic prose and embrace idiom. Likewise, historian and *New Yorker* contributor Jill Lepore (as cited in Nelson, 2016) called on scholars to tell stories, which, Lepore believed, can communicate arguments; stronger yet, unlike conventional academic argumentation, stories make people care about arguments.

However, before we tackle the question of how exactly to turn facts and arguments into stories, we need to consider a more elementary problem: how to answer a question so that our responses do not inadvertently become a minilecture. Again, insight into the limitations within which editors and journalists operate can help us deliver our knowledge in quotes that are potentially usable to them and satisfying to us. Unlike our writings, which typically comprise many thousands of words, most news articles must make their point in 600 to 1,200 words. Public radio interviews typically allow for the most airtime, and television interviews often allow for the least. At one end of the spectrum are the very tight constraints when reporters must obtain 1- or 2-minute clips for television or insert one, at most two, succinct quotes into a story. At the other end of the spectrum, reporters for public radio and affiliates might be able to interview at their leisure (20–30 minutes) because interviews are pre-recorded and answers can be edited if they are too long. Even then, it is often in one's best interest to keep answers relatively brief and let the reporter chime in regularly and ask questions. The exception to the rule, I have found, is when you're being interviewed for stories that specifically focus on your research or when you sense a synergy with the reporter; in these cases, I will let myself speak longer before pausing—a couple of paragraphs rather than a couple of sentences.

In other words, we need to learn how to tell a story for an audience that, unlike our students, doesn't need a grade that depends on decipher-ing 50 minutes of twists and turns. Our stories—and the moral of those stories—need to be conveyable in a reporter's paragraph. How can we do that without sacrificing the integrity of scholarship and the scientific process? As suggested earlier, the first rule is to be crystal clear on what we think. With clarity, it becomes easier to choose that one personal story and select those one or two statistics that exemplify the core of our message. It also becomes much easier to leave out the trappings of our professional training: the methodological and theoretical contributions and the hedg-ing on the exact claims in our work. We start with the main finding and its significance and add context later, as needed, rather than vice versa. Indeed, we might heed the words of George Balanchine, as he goaded his performers to shine to their fullest: "What are you saving it for? Do it now!" Leading with our key message, however, is not enough. We have to make it come alive for our intended audience. It should speak directly and in some tangible way to the concerns, questions, and realities of their world—whether it be the world of policymakers, parents, or practitioners (Schalet, Tropp, & Troy, 2017). For some researchers, making the message come alive is easy: Qualitative researchers are usually adept at linking abstract analyses with concrete instances. Quantitative researchers might use anecdotes from their everyday life or study participants to illustrate general principles. Researchers who study things, not people, can also tell compelling stories; for example, physical chemist Scott Auerbach advised: "See how stories are created and how hooks are written. Notice how the story is about human problems, with technology as a means to an end, but the story is ultimately not about technology" (personal communication, September 20, 2016).

Adept storytellers employ all the weapons in their arsenal, including metaphor, humor, idiom, catchy questions, and emotion (Baron, 2010; Pinker, 2014). Here, it is worth addressing the concern that using such weapons could violate the impartiality required for the scientific process. It need not. That said, a good research story does usually imply a call to action, and it is worth taking time to consider the practical implications of our message. In my experience communicating with nonacademic publics and guiding others to do the same, I have found that scholars do best when they decide what implications they can stand behind and then practice stating practical or policy implications clearly and concisely. Doing so increases the likelihood that reporters will tell the story that you are hoping they will. If you are not clear about the implications of your message, others' dictates may well stick with readers or viewers longer than will your words. And though it takes practice, it is certainly possible to at once exercise caution and respect for the scientific process and articulate takeaway messages that readers and viewers can use in their lives (Schalet et al., 2017).

PREPARING FOR THE INTERVIEW

With greater clarity about the content and implications of your message, you will be better equipped to share your expertise with journalists and reporters. One of the best ways to prepare for speaking with reporters is to regularly speak about your research with nonacademics, or at least those who do not share your discipline. Sadly, it is possible to successfully graduate from a PhD program, gain tenure, and become a full professor without ever having been required to communicate about research with anyone other than peers. Not surprisingly, then, we find ourselves either without words or overly wordy when first trying to talk about the general significance of what we do—not an ideal way to go on air. The good news is that it is often quite easy to set up a gig speaking about one's research to nonacademics. Myriad professional and practitioner organizations are eager to learn from research specialists about topics related to their programs and practice. A local library or public school might also be eager to line up a speaker from a nearby university. Cross-professional, community, and even interdisciplinary speaking opportunities can help clarify our thinking and interrupt our normal, jargon-laden speech. Beyond allowing us to hone our presentation skills, these encounters with new audiences— inside and outside of academia—will often give us perspectives on our research that can strengthen our mastery of the field. Particularly when audiences have their own source of knowledge about the topic we study, we have much to learn from them.

When I was a freshly minted PhD, I had the good fortune to obtain a postdoc in a medical school. There, I learned that I needed to say much less than I was accustomed to in my sociology training to convince my medical colleagues that my research was legitimate. But I had to say much more than I learned in sociology about how my research in the area of adolescent sexuality might pertain to other concrete issues relevant to adolescent health and well-being. In particular, I had to learn to speak to my new colleagues' questions about how my research showing that normalizing conversations between adults and teens to promote adolescent sexual health could help inform their practice—from office décor to patient intake to grant proposals. At first, I had little to say about those things and took my cues from my colleagues, who enthusiastically suggested how they might change protocols, hang new posters, and frame their research questions for funding agencies. Eventually, I learned from them, and many others at conferences to which I would later be invited to speak, to use this dialogue to think together about how to responsibly extrapolate from what I knew to what we might know and do. I also learned a great deal of relevant information that enhanced my expertise and familiarized me with the consensus and cutting-edge research in allied fields, such as public health and psychology.

All of this knowledge stood me in good stead for writing opinion editorials for national newspapers years later and for responding without blinking an eye to a CNN interviewer's question about Gardasil (the vaccine protecting against human papillomavirus and cervical cancer). My ability to respond was certainly the result of these years of engaging in very beneficial cross-professional dialogue with physicians (see also Chapter 9, this volume). Indeed, my experience certainly confirmed Barbara Ehrenreich's other point in her journalist's plea—namely, that none of the great problems we face in society today are the purview of one discipline and that to speak knowledgeably about these problems, we do well to take note of what our colleagues in allied disciplines are saying. This does not mean spending years becoming an interdisciplinary scholar, though becoming an adept public communicator does, I believe, require some time across disciplines and professions and familiarizing oneself with highly relevant current events.

One's key job, however, when preparing for a media appearance is not to gather more information. The formidable challenge is to shrink down what one already knows into three to five main points one decides to make. Those main points cannot have additional codicils, like an a, b, or c. Instead, these talking points should be able to stand on their own and be ones that you know by heart before conversing with a reporter. You might find it useful to think of these talking points as the things you want to make sure to have said, the mental checklist to go down, when a reporter ends by asking, "Is there anything else readers should know?" For me, they are the security blanket that gives me the freedom to think and talk on my feet, and do so creatively. Off camera, talking points can be printed out and in one's full view. On camera, with the pressure of a short, live recording, knowing your talking points by heart gives you the confidence that, amid angst, there are a few important things you really do know for sure.

Unless the news story itself is a scientific breakthrough of a highly technical nature (which is rare in social science), theory and method have no place in talking points. Moreover, researchers are under no obligation to have their talking points cover all the main points of their journal article, book, or even the abstract in question. It is perfectly permissible to leave out key parts of the theoretical argument, as long as one does not leave out information that could result in mischaracterization of the findings or misleading conclusions. In other words, it is possible that we will leave out some of the things that most interest us about our research when communicating with audiences that do not have the time or context to understand what intrigues us in relation to scholarly conversations. For it is those audiences that we must keep in mind when constructing our talking points: Although we do want to establish rapport, our job is not to make the reporter happy. Our job is to communicate what we think is important for the consumer of the media to know. When preparing talking points, ask yourself: What should a parent of a teenager, a young person, a teacher, a pediatrician, a policymaker, or even a voter take away from this? Ideally, the talking points include an action that follows from the knowledge and is doable. For instance, my talking point was about keeping conversations about sex open between parents and teens (CNN, 2011); a colleague in chemistry once focused on limiting total intake of rice and rice products to less than two cups, uncooked, a week (Tyson, 2015).

Finally, preparing for an interview requires practicing how to redirect and reframe questions so that you can be confident about being able to return to your points no matter the question. Learning how to bridge, as some communication experts call this technique, does not require you to sound like a politician or a broken record. It is much more akin to taking a question from a student who is coming out of left field and briefly addressing her or his immediate concern before segueing into the answer you believe the student needs to hear. In other words, we can learn to redirect questions we don't want to fully engage in a way that is educational and illuminating and does not make the reporter (or the viewer or listener) feel ignored or shamed. Many universities have media relations staff who are willing to help one practice such redirections, and if one has the funds, it can certainly be useful to employ the services of communication specialists, particularly if they are experienced at working successfully with researchers. In a pinch, a colleague or even a friend can be immensely helpful by asking a few direct and hard mock questions, with a stopwatch in hand.

THE INTERVIEW

Keep in mind there is no one prototypical interview. Speaking to reporters varies by medium, by live or prerecorded taping in the case of radio and TV, and also, importantly, by whether reporters are driven by purely commercial motives or by a set of value commitments to the topic at hand. Interviews also vary depending on whether you are being invited to comment on a current event or whether your work is the news. You want to know beforehand where an interview falls, so that you can plan your talking points accordingly. On a high-stakes television or radio program, generally you will have a preinterview or an informal phone conversation first—sometimes with the person who will be doing the interview but often with an assistant who will convey to the interviewer what they think are the most important points. In my experience, unless the person conducting the preinterview is the same as the person who will be speaking with you on air, there may be little overlap between the preinterview and the real interview, so it is best not to count on being asked the same questions again.

You can do a couple of things right to set the stage for optimal chemistry. A key one involves establishing rapport with the interviewer—and, by proxy, with the audience. On camera, it is essential to smile and to make eye contact with the interviewer. This is infinitely easier to do in person than in a remote studio, but even in the latter case, try to smile into the camera (and envision an audience of actual people behind the lens). Establishing a connection with the interviewer, before talking, will also ground you in the moment. For on-camera interviews, we should present ourselves at our best: Attractive and professional dress, blues or soft tones, without distracting prints, are ideal. If you are being filmed on-site, you will likely have the opportunity to be groomed and made up by professionals. When filmed off-site, you might consider going to a professional groomer or getting help with makeup. For radio, interviews will typically require a trip to the closest professional broadcasting facilities. I try to arrive at least 15 minutes early to become accustomed to the room, test the microphone, read over my notes, take a few deep breaths, and do a few stretches. I prefer to stand for radio interviews, as I find it easier to breathe deeply from the belly, which can help steady nerves, and because standing makes me feel more confident than does speaking into a microphone while seated.

For interviews that are anything other than live recordings, it can be helpful to establish several things beforehand. Specifically, you want to know whether the interview is being recorded or if the reporter will be taking notes from which they will be reconstructing quotes. In the latter case, you want to be especially careful to speak somewhat slowly and pause regularly. You will also want to know whether you will be allowed to look at the story before it is published. Generally that will not be the case, but sometimes reporters will allow you to read portions of the story and, importantly, to verify and fact-check your quotes. Some reporters are understandably averse to showing stories or even quotes to their sources before they are published because the latter might be tempted to change what they said after a story has been written and has moved through editorial process. That said, news outlets are very sensitive about getting factual information absolutely current and correct, and if they don't and you let them know, they will place corrections after publication, which every journalist wants to avoid.

My experience is that if you are speaking with a reporter who is a professional—and is either neutral or sympathetic toward the research you're sharing—and if you have distilled and reiterated your message, the news stories will accurately reflect your main findings and insights. However, specifics can inadvertently get lost in translation, especially when we get technical. Try to use language or visual aids to clarify statistics, so that there can be no misunderstanding about what a given percentage or proportion refers to; for instance, "two out of three" is better than "67 per-cent." During or at the end of the interview, you can also ask the reporter to tell you what they are taking away from what you've said so far and double-check that what they have taken in is what you meant. Education professor Walter Secada (personal communication, September 26, 2016) advised academics to follow up interviews with a short e-mail restating the main takeaways and to post a short summary of the research on one's webpage for anyone wanting to verify the research conclusions.

In my interviews, I have frequently encountered two challenges—related to causality and controversy—that can lead to misinterpreta-tion and mischaracterization of one's research. To illustrate how I have addressed these challenges, I draw on my CNN interview. As a social sci-entist, I was trained to be very careful around making so-called causal statements—in other words, statements that assert that one thing in the social world leads to another. Imagine my horror when I showed up to the CNN green room (where you are left to wait and stew in your nerves once you've been made up and groomed) at 8 a.m. on the Friday after Christ-mas and heard the CNN newscaster cheerfully state, "Do teen sleepovers prevent pregnancy? One researcher says yes and explains why." My book, *Not Under My Roof: Parents, Teens and the Culture of Sex*, about which I would shortly be interviewed, centers on the practice of parents permit-ting teenage couples to sleep together at home in the Netherlands, where the teen birth rate is one of the lowest in the world. The causal story is complex, and I knew I could easily waste my 5 precious minutes detail-ing why the title the editors chose was incorrect. Instead, I waited for the right opportunity during the interview to state simply that many things contribute to the low Dutch teenage birth rates, including a much lower poverty rate in the Netherlands than in the United States and better access to health care services. The general cultural climate around teenage sexu-ality that my book highlights also plays a role. After all, when a teenager feels she can confide in a parent and make an appointment with a doctor, she will be more likely to prevent a pregnancy when she starts having sexual intercourse. In short, I was able to correct the inaccurate causal claim while reaffirming my main message: that open parent–teen communication about sexuality and relationships is paramount for adolescent health.

Similarly, I was prepared for—and therefore able to deflect—a reaction of outrage or the possibility of being pigeonholed as a crazy foreigner (I have a Dutch accent) or liberal college professor trying to get parents in the heartland to let their teenage children have sex at home. Indeed, after the camera turned off, the interviewer turned to me and said, "When I first heard about your book, I thought the idea was complete insanity, but now I see that it makes sense." I think the interview went so well because when the interviewer and I met for a minute before the cameras went on, I shook his hand, smiled, and locked eyes, inviting him to view me not as a person with crazy ideas but as a regular human being. And throughout the interview I returned to my main talking points, which had been honed over many conversations with youth-serving professionals, pivoting away from extremity to a simple intuitive message: This is not about sleepovers; it is about parents and teenagers staying connected and kids not feeling a need to sneak around. Parents who have open conversations about sex and romance can better maintain that connection and help their kids stay healthy. As one of my coaches later said gleefully, "By the end of the interview you had him talking like you."

CONCLUSION

By drawing on the principles outlined in this chapter and optimizing our research expertise and pedagogical skills, we can, I believe, accomplish a great deal more in our exchanges with the media. To do so, we must see the interviewer or reporter as a real person to whom we are relating as people. We need to acknowledge and honor their perspective, even as we use our expertise to shift their understanding. We won't ever tell the whole story, but we can tell the most important part of the story for the audiences we want to reach. Doing so successfully does not require us to stay strictly on one given script. For if we are well prepared, the questions that do come out of left field can be opportunities to improvise, learn more, and foster a richer educational media conversation.

REFERENCES

Baron, N. (2010). *Escape from the ivory tower: A guide to making your science matter.* Washington, DC: Island Press.

CNN. (2011, December 26). *Do teen sleepovers prevent pregnancy: One researcher says yes and explains why* [Video file]. Retrieved from http://am.blogs.cnn.com/2011/12/26/do-teen-sleepovers-prevent-pregnancy-one-researcher-says-yes-and-explains-why

Ehrenreich, B. (2007). A journalist's plea. In D. Clawson, R. Zussman, J. Misra, N. Gerstel, R. Stokes, D. L. Anderton, & M. Burawoy (Eds.), *Public sociology* (pp. 231–238). Berkeley: University of California Press.

Nelson, M. K. (2016, February). *Is there a future for creative writing in academia?* Retrieved from http://www.megankatenelson.com/is-there-a-future-for-creative-academic-writing-in-academia

Pinker, S. (2014, September 26). Why academics stink at writing. *The Chronicle Review.* Retrieved from http://www.chronicle.com/article/Why-Academics-Writing-Stinks/148989

Schalet, A. (2016, August 18). Should writing for the public count toward tenure? *The Conversation.* Retrieved from https://theconversation.com/should-writing-for-the-public-count-toward-tenure-63983

Schalet, A. T., Tropp, L. R., & Troy, L. M. (2017). *A relational model for public engagement: Making research usable.* Manuscript in preparation.

Tyson, J. (2015, May 7). Are we eating too much arsenic? We need better tests to know. *The Conversation.* Retrieved from https://theconversation.com/are-we-eating-too-much-arsenic-we-need-better-tests-to-know-40732

Wai, J., & Miller, D. (2015, December 1). Here's why academics should write for the public. *The Conversation.* Retrieved from https://theconversation.com/heres-why-academics-should-write-for-the-public-50874

3

The Public: Engaging a Nonscholarly Audience

Samuel R. Sommers

We take idiosyncratic paths on the journeys that lead us to our disciplinary destination of psychology. Some of us are initially inspired by an engaging professor in an introductory course; some of us read an article or book that provides a new conceptual lens for a question we previously pondered. But a common unifying theme to these origin stories is the appeal of psychology as the science of everyday life: Most of us relish the opportunity to engage with the marvels of daily human experience.

Not that we're the only ones. At least, we psychologists are often inclined to assume (perhaps arrogantly) that our field is inherently interesting to pretty much anyone who hears about it—that but for their past misfortune of not having crossed paths with the right professors, articles, or books, most people we know might have become psychologists themselves. And that we're lucky they didn't, because now we get to be the ones

http://dx.doi.org/10.1037/0000066-004
Making Research Matter: A Psychologist's Guide to Public Engagement, L. R. Tropp (Editor)

to introduce them to the excitement of it all—in the classroom, through published papers, or at the occasional cocktail party.[1]

Of course, even once we enter the field, we take divergent roads as psychologists, devoting our time in different proportions to research, teaching, mentoring, service, clinical work, editorial duty, policymaking, grant writing, consulting, and more. Many of these professional amblings lead us to interact with audiences outside of academia. And—at least for those who would be drawn to read a chapter such as this one—these interactions can also inspire musings about writing for the broader public. Such thoughts inevitably raise tough questions—ones for which our graduate and early career training rarely provide much guidance.

In this chapter, I aim to identify and answer some of these most pressing questions regarding writing for a general audience. This is a daunting task for several reasons, not the least of which is that others in the field have written for the public for longer and with more success than I have. So I did what any good writer (or scientist) would do when faced with a formidable challenge: I asked for help. Specifically, I posed the following, straightforward query to more than two dozen colleagues: *What's your advice for psychologists considering writing for the general public?* Their answers, in the form of personal communications, are interspersed throughout the pages that follow, offering a generous panoply of insights on a range of relevant considerations. (In case you would like to check out the oeuvre of this panel of experts, a notable book by each is listed in the Suggested Readings section at the end of the chapter.)

First, a caveat: I gathered these quotes at a stage of my career when I was writing general-audience or trade books. Not everyone who reads this chapter will be pondering a project of similar scale. There are, of course, many other forms of writing for the broader public, including articles, op-eds, and blogs. Naturally, the logistics and mechanics of each differ; perhaps the best sources of guidance regarding these specifics are friends, colleagues, and mentors who have tried each form before. But my hope is

---

[1] To the extent that you go to cocktail parties. It seems like something an academic should do. I admit that I don't, but "cocktail party" reads better than "in the stands at a youth soccer game" or "over pizza at the bulk shopping store."

that this chapter will be helpful for those considering all types of general-audience writing, though I focus on the book in my case study.

SHOULD I DO IT?

Naturally, the first question is whether to tackle the endeavor in the first place. As we psychologists tend to do, allow me to answer the question with another question: Why are you considering it? If your answers include "Because I want to be famous," "Because I want to make a lot of money," or "Because I want to meet Stephen Colbert," then perhaps you should reconsider. When it comes to books, most aren't best-sellers, the pay rate might disappoint you when calculated down to the hourly level, and no talk show host reigns forever. More important, although I'm sure that some good books, blogs, and op-eds have been born from such motivations, I'd hypothesize that far more of them have grown out of smart people's feeling that they had something smart to say that would capture the interest of other smart people.

> If you're asking yourself, "what should I write a book about?" The answer is nothing. You should be *inspired* to write a book . . . a book should be welling up inside you to get out.
>
> —Dan Gilbert

Gilbert's assertion is fascinating as well as—by his own admission—a bit contrarian. One could read it as deriving from the divine-intervention school of thought, implying an intimidatingly high standard for the decision to take the plunge, not to mention an underestimation of the effort required to complete it (à la the famed songwriter who claims that the hit song "just came to me one day" and "practically wrote itself"). But Gilbert is really making a less controversial point: One should write because one has something to write, not because the title "author" has a nice ring to it. The same applies to titles like "blogger" and "op-ed columnist."

I think Gilbert's advice can also be read with a sigh of relief. We psychologists are regularly inspired by human behavior—living it, researching it, trying to understand it. We are fortunate to study the familiar and the accessible and to do so in creative and sometimes counterintuitive ways. To be blunt, our colleagues in other fields aren't always as lucky. There's good reason that our institutions often send prospective students, parents, and alumni visitors in our direction to sit in on psychology courses. These classes almost always offer a topic that intelligent laypeople can relate or respond to. I won't go so far as to suggest that every research study in our field is a book waiting to be written. But within almost every psychological research program lies an engaging story to be told.

> Media articles provide a great pilot test: An opportunity to see if people beyond your lab are interested in the kind of work you're doing, and to see if *you* are interested in doing the work required to communicate with a broader audience.
>
> —Liz Dunn

It is important to emphasize that these engaging stories that our research wants to tell need not come in book form. The op-ed, the popular magazine article, and the guest blog post all constitute fruitful testing grounds as well as worthwhile endeavors in and of themselves. Sometimes invitations for these submissions arise organically, as when you publish academic papers that attract the attention of others. But there's no reason to wait for a request to fall into your lap. You can work with the public relations department at your institution or the media affairs staff of your professional society. You can get in touch with colleagues and friends who have written similar pieces, asking for their suggestions as well as potential contacts. You can even submit to many outlets directly, without anyone knowing that you've done so—though, as with grants, journal articles, and job applications, it's much easier to miss the mark when you don't first solicit feedback or investigate what the evaluator's particular expectations are.

And even if you decide that, yes, there is an audience out there for your work and, yes, you might have a knack for writing for it, you should also consider whether you'll be comfortable doing so. Later, this chapter explores in detail the differences between academic and general-interest writing. But for now, I relay the insightful words of another colleague, who captures one of the major philosophical tugs-of-war inevitably encountered when writing for the broader public (again, a dilemma to which we will return shortly):

> Deciding whether to talk about your research with the general public is an important and complex decision. Are you comfortable if the public gets the gist of the scientific truth but loses 15% of the nuance? Or is that something that will upset you?
>
> —Eli Finkel

HOW SHOULD I START?

So let's say you've decided that writing for a broader audience is something you'd like to try. Let's also say you have some idea of what you'd like to write about and where you'd like to publish it. What's next? Probably refinement of the idea. Because if your answer to "What's your book (or op-ed or blog post) about?" is "my research," then there's still work to be done. Fortunately, many of the authors I contacted suggested that much of this work comes in the enjoyable form of simply having conversations with other people.

> Write about things that your smart aunt or uncle would find interesting—that you could talk about at a dinner party without putting people to sleep in two minutes.
>
> —Mike Norton (with Liz Dunn)

> Talking to people outside the field is incredibly helpful for two reasons. First, it is a wonderful way to remain grounded and answer the question of "am I studying something important that is relevant to people in the 'real world'?" Second, it is a great way to figure out how to best communicate ideas so that you get the person's attention and raise their appetite for more.
>
> —Francesca Gino

In short, workshop your ideas with your target audience: other intelligent people. When hitting the academic job market, many of us were advised to hone an elevator speech, the brief but compelling description of what we "do" in terms of research. So should it be for your general-audience writing as well. For a shorter work, the elevator speech might be the gist of what you ultimately write. For a book, it will prove helpful in organizing your thoughts for the written proposal, and it will be essential for pitching the book to potential agents, editors, or—once it's written—members of the media.

More good news: Other work you need to do is also painless. Namely, you need to:

> Read A LOT of general-audience writing in your area. Find the writing you like, and use that as a model.
>
> —Paul Bloom

Why is this such good advice? Because writing shares a great deal in common with two other enterprises to which I devote much of my time and energy: teaching and parenting. I mean this in the sense that most of what I have learned in these domains comes not from formal instruction but from observational learning and trial and error. When we start to teach, who among us doesn't draw upon fond memories of our own favorite teachers or liberally borrow from old activities and assignments? As students, sons, and daughters, don't we all compile mental checklists of the moves we swear we'll never make when we're on the other side of the desk or minivan? Writing feels much the same in terms of emulating and adapting—consciously or otherwise—effective techniques we've seen elsewhere, as well as learning to recognize what probably won't work as well for us.

HOW IS THIS WRITING DIFFERENT?

We've heard from authors about the importance of selecting a topic that will attract attention in a competitive marketplace, a less pressing consideration when publishing academically. Yet another recurring theme appears in the responses that they sent me: the expectations of the general-public reader.

> A problem is that the public wants clear, unambiguous, direct answers and explanations. Scientists are often uncertain and debate many issues,

> so scientific writing is full of caution and tentative generalization. To
> write for the general public it is necessary to overcome that habit.
>
> —Roy Baumeister

This brings us back to the tug-of-war between scientific precision and audience engagement. The regular reader of research journals might reasonably argue that we psychologists don't do clear, unambiguous, and direct all that well. In journal articles, we speak a language of probability-based analysis of multiply determined outcomes. Not "If X then Y," but rather "If X then a significantly increased likelihood of some degree more of Y."

Of course, the effort to obey both the masters of precision and engagement complicates more than just general-audience writing—it is a relevant topic for multiple chapters of this volume. Those of us who teach research methods encounter it when the naïve student, in the effort to create a more compelling paper, writes of "proving" a hypothesis to be true. Our media interviews lead to headlines offering causal conclusions for nonexperimental data. In my experience as an expert witness, cross-examination—and even direct testimony—frequently presents a tightrope of remaining faithful to the science while also offering easily digestible responses. For these (and other) reasons, I'd propose that these are crossover skills: Practice and success with teaching, media appearances, and consulting make one better suited for general-interest writing. And vice versa.

> In journal articles we are always trying to convince the reader that
> the research is done right. The general audience reader assumes the
> research is done right. She wants to know why it matters.
>
> —Keith Payne

Indeed, an implied expertise is bestowed upon the author who writes an op-ed or publishes a trade book (and the researchers whose work is described therein). Sure, a savvy reader will question the details of a particular study or its generalizability, but these responses are outliers. Some authors may view this experience—as liberating, freeing them from familiar concerns about methodological detail and statistical nuance and enabling a focus on big picture and implication.

I also find it daunting.[2] With a journal submission, we come to expect that eagle-eyed expert reviewers will inevitably send us more than what seems like a fair share of prepublication critique, correction, and alternative explanation—whether we want it or not (and in some cases, in enough quantity to prevent us from ever getting past prepublication status). General-audience authors proceed without such a formalized checkpoint: For a book, there will be some fact-checking and vetting from the publisher's legal department but no built-in peer review (for a blog, you're really flying solo). Although that may sound appealing, it also means operating without a safety net, unless you create your own (and you should; I remain indebted to those colleagues and friends whom I have roped into peer-review duty over the years).

> The issue of practical implications for the reader strikes me as centrally important to a successful trade book. These readers are much less likely to be concerned with the *hows, whens,* or *whys* in our material as by the *therefores* in it.
>
> —Bob Cialdini

An additional difference is that when it comes to a trade book, an emphasis on takeaways infuses almost every conversation you will have about your work. As Cialdini noted, the how, when, and why of each study described inevitably take a backseat. Somewhat ironically, this means these same words also tend to find their way into our general-audience book titles, in such forms as *The Science of Doing A,* or *Why We Always B,* or *How to Get Better at C,* in the effort to demonstrate that reading them will translate into immediate and quantifiable gains. In short, here I am not simply talking about writing for an audience with a different level of familiarity with your topic. I am also talking about writing for an audience with a very different set of motivations and expectations for reading.

---

[2] Especially when describing the research of others, which elicits feelings of heightened obligation to do justice to it and to do so accurately.

HOW DO I DO THIS?

On this question, the major theme to emerge from our consulting authors' advice was that of changing well-learned habits. Not that the tendencies we rely upon when writing journal articles are bad habits—they're adaptive for navigating that particular audience. But different audiences require different approaches.

> Forget everything you know about the subject. The biggest impediment to writing for a lay audience is the inability to overcome one's expert perspective and understand how an ordinary reader will hear your words.
>
> —Dan Gilbert

It is an apparent contradiction—or at least, a frustration—that many of us have encountered from both directions: The more expert we become at a particular skill or pursuit, the more difficult it tends to be to explain it to others. This so-called curse of expertise has been observed among a range of practitioners, from electricians to athletes, and its causes include a certain amnesia regarding our own mental state back when we were novices. Teachers and authors are not exempt. Although some (perhaps even ourselves, self-deprecatingly) may malign us with the axiom "Those who can't do, teach," we are experts in our particular domains. And the act of educating—whether in the classroom or via the written word—is fraught with the same risks as other efforts to convey expertise across boundaries.

> I learned that I wrote best when I imagined myself speaking to an audience rather than writing a book.
>
> —Mahzarin Banaji

> Write as if it were a chatty letter to friend. You can make it more formal in editing if needed.
>
> —Dick Nisbett

How to solve this problem? I reserve for the final section of this chapter concrete solutions and how-to options. But as the preceding advice illustrates, from the standpoint of a more general writing philosophy, reimagining the entire task is often called for. A letter to a friend, a colloquium rather than an article, a conversation not a manuscript—whether via these or other reconceptualizations, much can be gained by thinking of writing for a general audience as a qualitatively different enterprise from your past writing efforts.

There's irony here, in that previous writing is often what puts us in the position to embark upon this new endeavor. Our experience with academic writing is nothing to hide, but assumptions and tendencies must be overcome. And yet, there remain aspects of academic publishing we should want to bring with us across boundaries and to the broader public, as wisely noted by Tavris's advice:

> Model the key themes of scientific and critical thinking: that what we know is inseparable from how we know it; that opinions must be based on evidence; that not all opinions have equal validity; and that science gives us probabilities—only pseudoscience gives us certainties.
>
> —Carol Tavris

Again, this is a daunting task: Remain true to methodological and philosophical roots as scientists, but do so in an engaging, conversational, and accessible manner. It isn't easy. But as it is said: If it were, everyone would do it.

BUT SPECIFICALLY, HOW DO I DO THIS?

On this question, our published colleagues sent many specific suggestions, including strategies I had never considered as well as others that I had stumbled upon myself but had never before managed to articulate so clearly. So without further ado, allow me to get out of the way and present a lightly annotated compendium of concrete strategies for writing for the general public.

> Try to hook the reader's interest quickly—for example, by saying something paradoxical, or something that addresses a puzzle or

problem or need that many people are thinking about. Avoid the twin perils of opening in a sensationalistic or pedestrian way.

—Jonathan Haidt

Bob Cialdini (whom we heard from earlier, and will hear from again shortly) seconded Haidt's sentiment, noting that when he reads through scientific trade books, he finds that the most successful sections typically begin with a puzzle. Ideally, it is a puzzle that grabs attention in the manner of the detective story or other mystery, such that readers would actually feel psychological discomfort if they had to put down the book before getting resolution.

> I try not to state anything in abstract terms before providing an illustration (the more realistic, the better). . . . If you're describing research it will almost certainly be more understandable if you describe it from the subject's perspective, rather than the researcher's.
>
> —Tony Greenwald (with Mahzarin Banaji)

Yet another helpful reminder of the importance of getting into the mind of your audience.

> Small words are good. Simple sentences, too. Forget what your third-grade teacher taught you about never starting a sentence with *but* or *and*. They are so much better than *however* and *moreover*. But don't overdo it.
>
> —Keith Payne

Brilliant.

> Abandon that stodgy, imperious, uninvolved narrator who lives for jargon, precision, and the passive voice, and start writing in the same voice in which you teach your undergraduates. Indeed, don't *write* to readers. Talk to them!
>
> —Dan Gilbert

Echoing these pieces of advice is perhaps the best compliment I've ever received for my writing: "When I read your book, it really sounded like your voice talking." That's what you're striving for when writing for a general audience. There's an intimacy with the reader available via this type of writing that we don't experience with journal articles. But bear in mind, this doesn't mean that every psychology op-ed or trade book should sound the same. After all, we each use different voices when we teach, and we each have different levels of comfort with intimacy.

> Get sharp and critical people to look over your work before submitting. Pay special attention to comments or concerns that more than one person has. Remember the Yiddish saying: *If one man calls you a donkey, ignore him. If two men call you a donkey, think about it. If three men call you a donkey, buy a saddle.*
>
> —Paul Bloom

Humor often helps. And if you don't feel that humor is in your writer's toolbox, other means of eliciting an emotional response from the reader can accomplish similar objectives.

> Don't write in your university office, which is full of cues likely to prime a certain vocabulary, style, and way of communicating information. Instead, write from a coffee shop or a place at home with a window overlooking a street with passersby. They're your intended audience after all.
>
> —Bob Cialdini

Again, brilliant.

There is also the question of the right time to try this. Psychology remains a field centered on publishing journal articles. Because of the zero-sum nature of a daily calendar, writing for the broader public comes at the expense of time spent on other ventures that are more directly tied to finding, keeping, and being promoted within a tenure-track position. Everyone's experiences are different, but I set about writing the sample chapter and proposal for my first general-audience book the summer after submitting my tenure application. At that juncture, it seemed a not-completely-irresponsible time to dabble in a new adventure. Even just one semester earlier, it would have felt (to me, at least) like a foolhardy pursuit.

Don't get me wrong: It still felt foolhardy. Alone behind a locked office door, working on a project that no one really knew about—and during the proposal stage, a project about which it was possible that no one would ever know—the entire experience seemed a bit like playing make-believe in private. It continued to feel that way for many prepublication months thereafter. I recommend some of the advice offered earlier in this chapter: Start small. In my case, that meant first some time spent blogging on a popular website, which provided me with excellent trial-and-error fodder for the ultimate book project.

There are also nuts-and-bolts considerations, such as how to start the process. When it comes to books, a nonfiction work (unlike a novel) need not be completed for a publisher to buy it (in fact, it usually isn't). But you will need at least one sample chapter; you will also need a book proposal.[3] And what might be the single most important piece of advice I received when embarking upon my first book—one that several of the authors I contacted echoed: You will want to find a literary agent. I presume exceptions to this rule must exist, but I can envision no other way in which pitching, selling, and publishing a book today is feasible.

How do you find this agent who will be the one to champion your book before it is a book? Agents are on the lookout for new authors: Yet another reason to write blog posts or an op-ed or give media interviews is that these might catch someone's eye and elicit an e-mail of interest. But you can also find an agent on your own. Browse their websites and pay special attention to stated genres of interest and the authors they already represent. Read the acknowledgments sections of other psychologists' books, in which you can usually find a thank you to the agents who brokered their deals. Once again, ask published authors for referrals.

If you submit to an agent, here's where your elevator speech comes in handy. Relay a concise and engaging summary of your book idea in your cover letter or e-mail. Identify comparable titles as well as what makes your project unique. Articulate clear, concrete lessons that readers can

---

[3] Plenty of other published resources exist to guide you through the mechanics of this process, so I do not devote space to them here. Published colleagues may also be willing to share the proposals out of which their eventual books grew.

expect to take from reading. Tout your platform and enthusiasm for publicizing a book. And remember that agents—like the editors who acquire books—aren't just looking at content. They're often swayed even more by how you write. Make sure your voice as an author shows through, in your proposal as well as in your sample chapters.

This marks yet another difference between writing for academics versus a general audience. With journals, we're used to navigating anonymous reviewers and editorial decision letters from a colleague. When writing for a general audience, be prepared for collaboration from the start from paid professionals with a different set of experiences, expectations, and incentives than yours. This interaction with agents and editors can—and hopefully will—do more than make your book possible: It will also make your book better. It can be challenging as well. Not all authors get much choice when it comes to landing an agent and editor. But if you do, shared vision is a key factor to weigh in the decision.

> Having a professional on board who really knows what you are trying to say will make the process so much easier in the long run. It's very hard to write a book when two of the key people have a different— even slightly different—book in mind.
>
> —Sam Gosling

CONCLUSION

On the topic of take-home messages, my hope would be that this chapter is full of them, mostly the kernels of wisdom shared by our author colleagues. But I also believe that the wide-ranging nature of their advice, in itself, offers lessons. First: There is no one way to write for the broader public. There is not a singular, elusive formula for success at finding an audience, hooking your readers, and maintaining their engagement for an entire op-ed or 200-plus book pages. This shouldn't be a surprise; there's also more than one way to give a great conference talk or teach a great class or carry out any of a number of tasks that we perform as psychologists.

Second, this type of writing need not be a solo venture. Admittedly, the act of writing involves an inherent solitude, in stereotype and in practice.

But much as this chapter has benefited immeasurably from the contributions of others, efforts to write for the general public are similarly enhanced by collaboration. Many of the authors whose advice can be found on the preceding pages have coauthored books (and op-eds and blog posts). Among those with solo bylines, most have written acknowledgment sections packed to the margins with gratitude for colleagues and editors who have read with a critical eye. I've done both, having published my first book on my own and my second with a (nonpsychologist) coauthor. The latter experience not only diffuses over two heads the pressure of completing the project but also allows for—at least the potential of—synergy born from two authors with complementary perspectives and approaches.

To end where I began, I'll note once more that we take idiosyncratic paths on the journeys that bring us to the field of psychology. It is much the same for those of us who meander down the avenue of writing for the broader public. And, thus, conversations with 30 different published authors are likely to yield (at least) 30 different (and sometimes competing) forms of advice. So if I may, allow me to close with one last tidbit of advice: Don't take too much advice. Seriously.

Consult a chapter or two like this one, sure. Talk with a few colleagues. Read more than a few of their published op-eds and blog posts and books. But that's enough. If you still feel the itch, stop pondering and start writing. When it comes to writing for a general audience, where can you find the best answers to the question of whether you should do it? Odds are, it's simply in seeing what happens when you sit down at that desk (or coffee shop table) and just give it a shot.

SUGGESTED READINGS

Banaji, M. R., & Greenwald, A. G. (2013). *Blindspot: Hidden biases of good people.* New York, NY: Delacorte.

Baumeister, R. F., & Tierney, J. (2011). *Willpower: Rediscovering the greatest human strength.* New York, NY: Penguin Press.

Bloom, P. (2013). *Just babies: The origins of good and evil.* New York, NY: Crown.

Cialdini, R. B. (1984). *Influence: The psychology of persuasion.* New York, NY: Morrow.

Dunn, E., & Norton, M. (2013). *Happy money: The science of smarter spending.* New York, NY: Simon & Schuster.

Finkel, E. (2017). *The all-or-nothing marriage: How the best marriages work.* New York, NY: Dutton.

Gilbert, D. (2006). *Stumbling on happiness.* New York, NY: Random House.

Gino, F. (2013). *Sidetracked: Why our decisions get derailed and how we can stick to the plan.* Boston, MA: Harvard Business Review Press.

Gosling, S. (2008). *Snoop: What your stuff says about you.* New York, NY: Basic Books.

Haidt, J. (2012). *The righteous mind: Why good people are divided by politics and religion.* New York, NY: Pantheon.

Nisbett, R. E. (2015). *Mindware: Tools for smart thinking.* New York, NY: Farrar, Straus and Giroux.

Payne, K. (2017). *The broken ladder: How inequality changes the way we think, live, and die.* London, England: Orion.

Sommers, S. (2011). *Situations matter: Understanding how context transforms your world.* New York, NY: Penguin.

Tavris, C., & Aronson, E. (2015). *Mistakes were made (but not by me): Why we justify foolish beliefs, bad decisions, and hurtful acts.* Boston, MA: Mariner Books.

4

Public Policy: How Psychologists Can Influence Lawmakers

Roberta Downing

In 2009, in the wake of the worst economic downturn since the Great Depression, the United States saw the emergence of a movement across the country of people who were focused on and angry about what they perceived to be excessively high federal spending and our growing national debt. The Tea Party movement, as it was called, began organizing protests and rallies not long after the inauguration of President Barack Obama. Those who participated in the movement opposed a number of actions taken by a Democratic majority in Congress, whether it was the stimulus bill of 2009 (i.e., the American Recovery and Reinvestment Act), which was passed to create jobs and help people negatively impacted by high unemployment and foreclosures; the Troubled Asset Relief Program, which was viewed by the Tea Party as a bailout of Wall Street; or the Affordable Care Act, which has since provided health insurance to millions of uninsured Americans. By the end of 2010, the movement had taken hold and was credited with

http://dx.doi.org/10.1037/0000066-005
Making Research Matter: A Psychologist's Guide to Public Engagement, L. R. Tropp (Editor)
Copyright © 2018 by the American Psychological Association. All rights reserved.

electing a new Republican majority to control the House of Representatives and state legislatures around the country.

As one of the most electorally effective grassroots campaigns in recent American history, the Tea Party provides an instructive example of citizen action that has effected change at the highest levels of government, achieved using two simple means: (a) knowing how to pressure lawmakers and (b) having the passion and energy to create change. The Tea Party has been fueled by people from a variety of professional and socioeconomic backgrounds—everyone from stay-at-home parents to schoolteachers to PhD-level scientists and billionaire owners of corporations. As evidenced by this movement, the power of American democracy lies in the fact that citizen action by regular, everyday people can yield incredible influence when they know how to work the political system, engage policymakers, and are willing to sustain the hard work needed to achieve their desired outcome.

Many psychologists yearn to use their research to influence policy but lack the knowledge of how to participate or effect change in this arena. Rarely are psychologists trained in how to engage or communicate with policymakers, and the professional incentives within the field do not usually reward psychologists for political engagement. Effecting policy change and making one's research relevant for elected officials are not usually criteria that help academic psychologists to achieve tenure or other tangible professional benefits. If anything, engaging in influencing policy could potentially take precious time away from research activities that serve as the main driving force underlying research psychologists' ability to advance their careers.

Still, many social scientists have been quite effective in making their research relevant for and accessible to policymakers. Economists' research is often cited by the media, which gets the attention of elected officials who then engage them. Economists also tend to work in policy-oriented think tanks more so than do psychologists (see Chapter 5, this volume). Other social scientists also frame their research questions around public policy debates, more so than do psychologists. In some psychology departments, applied or policy-relevant research is not explicitly valued or encouraged, whereas other disciplines (e.g., social workers, political scientists, economists) might base their entire body of research around an important public policy issue.

Yet psychologists have an enormous amount to offer policy debates. There is a policy issue for any number of psychological topics, whether it involves reform of the mental health system, discrimination in employment, affirmative action, police–community relations, dementia care and treatment, bullying, immigration, the need for federal research funding, obesity prevention, prison reform, or even issues such as climate change. Psychologists also have important skills to lend to policy debates. Policymakers make numerous arguments in favor of or in opposition to legislation, but the empirical basis behind these arguments is sometimes dubious. The arguments and talking points used by advocates and lobbyists are also often not rooted in empirical science. For example, when debating funding for food assistance programs in Congress, hunger advocates have consistently referred to how hunger affects children's academic performance, stating that children cannot concentrate at school when they are hungry. This point sounds like it is probably true and makes perfect sense as an argument. But, does the research show that hunger experienced by low-income children is a factor in their school performance? Is there evidence of this as a contributor or predictor of academic success or failure? What does the research say? Psychologists, with their understanding of research methods and statistical techniques and their access to research databases on a variety of topics, can provide the empirical data to support or reject a policy argument in ways that lay audiences are not necessarily equipped to do. National advocacy groups would welcome scientific research that backs up their talking points, and psychologists could add new arguments, based on scientific evidence related to the issue at hand. Advocacy groups and policymakers alike want to know what the research says but usually do not have access to it—and if they do, they might still need guidance regarding what conclusions can be drawn from the larger body of research.

In a series of steps, this chapter provides psychologists who are interested in engaging with policymakers with basic tools for engagement, with the goal of inspiring and motivating them to work to influence public policy and to disperse psychological findings broadly so they can effect the most policy change possible.

FIRST THINGS FIRST: HOW DOES THE POLICY SYSTEM WORK?

Whether one is operating at the federal, state, or local level, it is important to understand the structure of government, how it works, and who the players are. For example, who represents you at the city, state, and federal level? Depending on your geographic location, it can sometimes be easier to effect change at the local level by building relationships with your city councilperson, mayor, county executive, or governor.

In the case of the federal government, policy can be influenced at the level of the legislative (i.e., Congress), executive (i.e., the White House and federal agencies), and judicial branches of government. Psychological research has been used to influence congressional legislation and rule-making by federal agencies, as well as U.S. Supreme Court decisions for which the American Psychological Association (APA) submitted highly influential amicus briefs highlighting psychological research on topics such as same-sex marriage, segregation, and affirmative action.

Within the legislative branch of the federal government, it is important to understand the basic steps for legislation to become law. Bills are introduced by members of Congress. There are 100 U.S. senators (two per state) and 435 members of the House of Representatives. Bills are usually more successful if they are introduced on a bipartisan basis so that they have a champion from each party advocating for the bill's passage. However, it is not always possible to find bipartisan cosponsors for a bill. It is also helpful if a bill is introduced in both the House of Representatives and the Senate so it can move on dual tracks through both chambers. The more cosponsors that a bill has, the more successful it is likely to be because cosponsoring a bill indicates that a member would likely vote in favor of it should it come up for a vote. Some of the incremental work in advancing a bill over the years involves advocacy to urge more and more members to cosponsor a bill to build support for it.

Each bill that is introduced is referred to a committee of jurisdiction. Committees in the House of Representatives and Senate have different jurisdictions—for example, an education bill in the Senate would likely be referred to the Committee on Health, Education, Labor, and Pensions, whereas the same bill would be referred to the Education and the Workforce Committee in the House of Representatives. Bills usually have to pass committee to receive a vote on the floor, but some bills go straight to the House or Senate floor for a vote without committee consideration. There is limited time in each chamber of Congress to consider a bill on the floor, particularly in the Senate, so bills that receive floor votes are usually topics of national significance and can be highly political in nature. At any step in the process, a bill can stall because of political, procedural, and/or policy reasons. Indeed, the legislative process was set up to make it difficult to get bills passed by Congress so that only the most vetted and prioritized legislation becomes law.[1]

Advocating for a bill's passage can sometimes take years, but that does not mean that it is futile to engage. For example, many bills are considered "message bills"—their sponsors and the party that wants to advance them know that there is no chance of them becoming law because either the other chamber or the president has already indicated that they would not pass them. But the bill might still be brought to the floor for a vote to highlight the majority party's position on the topic or to put members on record in support of or in opposition to a particular issue. Thousands of bills that are introduced in every Congress are never acted upon at any

---

[1] Most bills that are brought to the Senate floor require 60 votes to prevent a filibuster, which is a parliamentary procedure often used by the minority party to continue debate on a bill and prevent or delay a vote. This 60-vote threshold can make it difficult to get a bill passed in the Senate. Even if a political party has a substantive majority, they still have to bring along some members of the other party to move their bill, which can be difficult with highly polarizing or contentious issues.

Noncontroversial bills can pass the Senate without a floor vote by using the procedural tactic of *unanimous consent*. When a bill is passed by unanimous consent, every Senate office is informed that a senator wants their bill passed and another senator has to actively block the bill to stop it from passing. If no one steps up to put a hold on it and block it, after a certain amount of time it passes the chamber without a vote. Many bills that are less political or noncontroversial in nature pass via this method. But any senator can block a bill that is advanced by this method, so to be successful, a bill has to not have any problems that might give any senator a reason to oppose it.

Bills can pass the House of Representatives with a simple majority vote. Legislation that has passed both the House and Senate is sent to the president for signature or veto. It takes a two-thirds vote in both chambers to override a presidential veto.

level. It is important to recognize that influencing policy is incremental and requires patience, determination, and endurance.

HOW CAN AN ACADEMIC LIKE ME INFLUENCE POLICYMAKERS?

At its most fundamental level, politics and policymaking in the local, state, and federal government are rooted in interpersonal relationships. This chapter is focused mostly on federal policy; however, the tactics that are discussed also apply to state and local government.

If you want to effect change at the federal level, one of the essential ways to influence policy is by developing long-term, ongoing relationships with the offices of your state's two U.S. senators and your representative in Congress. Members of Congress are interested in knowing what kind of research is being conducted in the state or congressional district that they represent. The academic institutions in a member's state or congressional district receive federal funding for research, and college students receive federal funding from Pell grants or federal student loans. Members of Congress and other public officials are interested in seeing how that federal funding is spent and the results it brings. They welcome researchers who visit them and explain their findings. Local policymakers welcome this kind of information as well. The importance of understanding and being engaged in public policy is particularly relevant for public institutions that in large part subsist on government funding.

How does one develop a relationship with one's member of Congress? There are a number of means for doing so. Psychologists can visit the Washington, DC office of their member of Congress any time that they might be in town for a conference or any other reason. It is as easy as picking up the phone, calling the congressional office, and asking to speak to the staff member who works on issues and legislation of interest to you. For example, psychologists who are interested in mental health issues would normally meet with and build a relationship with the health care staffer in the office. A psychologist who is interested in poverty and welfare issues might build a relationship with a different staffer who handles that portfolio of issues. When calling the office, you can ask the person who answers the phone for the name and e-mail address of the staffer who handles the issue in which you are interested and that person will connect you right away to that staffer. If the staff is not available to talk to you at that moment, you can leave a voicemail and follow up with an e-mail introducing yourself and asking for a meeting. You might end up meeting with the member of Congress, or you might meet with the staff. Often you can accomplish more by meeting and developing a relationship with the staff, as they do most of the legwork around the legislative issues.

If you are unable to go to Washington, DC, there are a number of ways to meet your member of Congress closer to home. Every senator and representative has a local office. You can look on the Internet to find out where they have a district office and then call that office and ask to meet with your member of Congress when they are in town. If they are unavailable to meet right away, you should ask to meet with a local (district or in-state) staff member. Developing a relationship with the staff is as important as developing a relationship with the member of Congress; it is a crucial part of the congressional staff's job to know what is going on in the member's district or state.

You never know what effects your research or a meeting with your member of Congress and/or their staff might have. There are many instances in which a researcher has visited their member of Congress to discuss an important finding from their work and that information is translated into a bill that the member of Congress introduces. Policymakers are always looking for new issues with which to engage and play a leadership role. Meeting with your local or federal policymaker to share your research may spark a new area of interest for them. The key, however, is to connect with the congressional staff not just once but on a regular basis. After meeting with staff, follow up with a thank-you note and keep the relationship going by meeting with the staff at least on an annual basis and sending the staff information that is relevant to the issue you discussed, whether in the form of a local newspaper article or newly published research. Think of ways to keep the connection going with the staff so that when an issue comes up that is relevant to your research, they will think of you as a resource and will reach out to ask for your insights or expertise related to the issue to inform the policymaker's decisions around it. Sometimes, once the staff know of your expertise, they may ask you to review a bill on that issue and provide them with feedback and suggestions that they may incorporate into the bill's language.

WHAT CHALLENGES MIGHT I ENCOUNTER IN WORKING WITH POLICYMAKERS?

Congressional offices tend to be understaffed because of budget constraints, and as a result, staff are overworked. Nonetheless, paid lobbyists and advocates are often persistent about engaging congressional offices to get their issues addressed. To remain relevant and make progress on your policy goals, it is essential that ongoing contact and relationships be maintained. Influencing public policy is about being the squeaky wheel that gets the attention. It takes time and does not happen overnight. But we have to participate unless we want other voices to speak for us.

Because of frequent staff turnover in congressional offices, you may end up working with several different staffers as you engage with the member over the years. Building relationships with whoever is handling the issue you are interested in is crucial to engaging the member of Congress over time. Members rely heavily on their staff and want the staff to be engaged with constituents, which is a major part of representing them in Congress. Members know that word gets around in their congressional districts and states and that when their office is responsive to constituents, others will hear about it back at home.

It is also important to understand that some staff and policymakers are more effective than others. Sometimes people become discouraged when trying to participate in the political process if the staff are hard to reach or are unresponsive. Or they become discouraged if a representative is from a political party that is different from their own. Despite these possibilities, it is still important to stay engaged with the congressional office and let them know when you agree or disagree with the vote a member takes, even if you feel it falls on deaf ears. There are members of Congress who might be politically or fiscally conservative but are still willing to protect programs from funding cuts or even invest in programs if they know they have constituencies in their district or state that would be negatively affected by funding cuts. You can never predict how a member may or may not be helpful on a topic until you ask for help with that issue.

Another challenge for academic psychologists is that the congressional calendar is quite different from the academic calendar. Some of Congress's busiest times are when the academic calendar is quiet. Congress, particularly in recent years, is highly driven by deadlines, whether those involve federal appropriations bills that must be passed to keep the government running or bills that must be reauthorized to avert significant harm. Some of Congress's busiest times are in June and July because Congress often needs to get certain legislative items completed before leaving Washington, DC for the month-long August recess as well as before the winter holidays. These times, usually slower for academic psychologists are when advocacy often needs to be ramped up.

WHAT CHANNELS CAN I USE TO REACH POLICYMAKERS?

You might use a variety of channels to connect with policymakers at the local, state, and federal levels. Oftentimes, members of Congress host public events you can attend—such as town halls or speeches that they give, either in their home district or in Washington, DC. Some senators hold "constituent coffees" in their Washington, DC office on a weekly basis so they can meet constituents who are visiting the city. Other members of Congress hold "Congress on your Corner" events in their congressional district where you can meet them in person, or they conduct conference calls you can join to hear about the congressperson's priorities and share your concerns. An option for psychologists working at a university is to invite your policymaker to the university to give a speech or host a roundtable with faculty and students. Speaking at public forums is an effective way to provide policymakers with a platform to discuss issues of common interest and policy ideas of relevance to the university and the community at large.

One of the key tools for influencing public policy is to read the news regularly and pay attention to how your member of Congress votes on issues. If your representative or senator votes in support of a bill and you have research evidence to share that is relevant to the issue, let them know. Conversely, if they vote in a way with which you disagree, let them know and present relevant research findings to explain why the vote they cast is at odds with empirical findings. You can also call, write, or tweet at your policymakers to influence them on a position ahead of a vote. Engaging ahead of as well as after a vote is crucial. Saying thank you for your vote or letting them know why you disagree with their vote is equally important. If a member votes in a way you disagree with, they need to know the ramifications of that vote. In this respect, it is particularly effective to point out how the member's vote aligns with the research on the topic or how the vote contradicted recommendations that are rooted in empirical research. Otherwise, the policymaker may assume that their constituents are not paying attention to that issue or that it is not important to their constituency. Being able to tell the member how their vote is or is not supported by the findings of empirical research is a special perspective that psychologists can bring to bear on particular topics.

Working with an advocacy group is another effective way to engage policymakers and use your research to influence legislation. A number of national advocacy groups based out of Washington, DC have local chapters. These national groups hold advocacy days on Capitol Hill on an annual basis and have legislative teams that inform people on their e-mail lists of the status of legislation in which the group is interested. Joining the activities of a national advocacy group is a useful way to develop relationships with policymakers because the advocacy groups follow legislation that is moving through Congress and can engage their membership around the country to weigh in with policymakers locally. The savvier advocacy organizations have a network of people throughout the country who work and lobby on a defined policy agenda. So, for example, if a member of Congress is wavering on a bill that is important to them, these groups call on their members who are constituents within that member's congressional district or state. Those advocates, who are voters that the member will listen to and who usually have long-standing relationships with their state's entire congressional delegation, activate their networks, who begin weighing in with the member's staff with phone calls, e-mails, tweets, or visits to their offices.

APA devotes significant resources to advocacy and provides resources for psychologists to engage with Congress. APA's Public Interest Directorate has a government relations team that conducts advocacy around social issues (e.g., women's issues; poverty; lesbian, gay, bisexual, transgender, and queer issues; juvenile justice; racial justice; immigration). APA's Science Directorate also has a government relations team that works on a number of research-related issues with Congress and the executive branch (e.g., support for research funding at federal agencies, informing scientific debates related to psychology specifically, peer review issues). APA's Education Directorate has a government relations team that works on issues such as support for graduate education, concerns related to student loans, early childhood and K–12 education, and the Higher Education Act. Additionally, APA's Practice Directorate works with Congress and the executive branch on issues such as reimbursement for practicing psychologists, mental health parity, and others related more specifically to mental health practitioners.

Psychological organizations such as the Society for the Psychological Study of Social Issues (SPSSI) and the Society for Research in Child Development (SRCD) also have developed policy expertise to help their members engage in influencing federal policy issues. Both organizations fund public policy fellowships, host congressional briefings, and provide their members with policy updates. Consortia such as the Consortium of Social Science Associations COSSA and the Federation of Associations in Behavioral and Brain Sciences (FABBS) advocate on issues of interest to psychologists. Given the resources these organizations provide, you don't need to "go it alone" when it comes to policy work and advocacy. Although your voice as an individual and constituent is important to lawmakers, and it is important to weigh in on issues with letters, phone calls, and the other mechanisms mentioned in this chapter, it is also very effective and perhaps less daunting and easier to engage by working with relevant professional associations. Many voices joined together from many different policy and research angles can often present the strongest case.

Other ways to use one's research to influence public policy is through the media (see Chapters 2 and 3, this volume). Writing an op-ed in a local newspaper about your research and its relevance to a policy issue is a highly effective way of making one's findings salient to policymakers. Policymakers and their staff at all levels of government scour both local and national newspapers every day. It is a major part of their job to stay abreast of current events both nationally and locally. Mentioning a policymaker's name in an op-ed that you have written in a local newspaper about a topic of concern is a highly effective way of making sure that they hear your message. Most policymakers and their staff have Google alerts set up so that they receive an e-mail any time that the policymaker's name is mentioned by the media. Writing an op-ed calling on a policymaker to vote or effect change in a particular way is a highly targeted means of getting a message across and influencing the broader debate.

There are also different levels of engagement with policymakers. If some of the ideas shared thus far seem daunting or too time-consuming, you can get started with smaller steps such as writing letters to your mayor, governor, or member of Congress about issues of concern to you. Policymakers have several staff devoted to answering constituent mail, and lawmakers want to know which issues their constituents are writing to them about. Writing a letter or e-mail is an important step toward other forms of engagement (e.g., in-person meetings). Calling your congressional office to weigh in with your opinion is another way of making your voice heard. The staff of congressional offices are accustomed to receiving calls from constituents on a range of issues. Everyone can and should call their elected officials to share their opinion as one of the most basic steps toward participating in our democracy. Furthermore, this is another way in which you can engage with an advocacy group to influence policy. Many advocacy groups, including APA, have action alerts that they send out to keep their members abreast of pertinent policy issues and ask their members to call or write to their member of Congress about a particular pressing issue. These advocacy groups will often draft the e-mail text for you and all you have to do is enter your contact information and an e-mail will be sent to the member from you. This is another type of engagement in which you do not have to necessarily go it alone and can work with groups that have the infrastructure to help guide you through the process or make it easy for you to engage.

ONCE I HAVE THEIR ATTENTION, HOW DO I COMMUNICATE WITH POLICYMAKERS?

One of the biggest challenges for academic researchers seeking to influence policy is how to translate research findings to make them meaningful for nonacademic audiences. Academic psychologists are accustomed to speaking with others who have a solid understanding of the field, theory, research methods, and statistics. However, when meeting with a congressional staffer, your city councilperson, or state representative, you may be talking to someone who has never taken a psychology course or statistics course or who has never undertaken postgraduate academic work of any kind. To be an effective communicator of psychological research, you must ensure that your comments and written materials are accessible to anyone of any background, with any level of education. It is also important to understand that policymakers often have a quite limited view of psychology, believing it to be mostly a field that diagnoses and treats mental illness. Few have an understanding of the very broad and diverse range of issues with which psychologists engage.

When meeting with a policymaker or their staff, explain your field—and your research in particular—and how you see your work relating to a particular issue. It is essential to be focused and have a specific agenda for these discussions. Drafting a fact sheet about your issue that fits on no more than one page of text is important to guide the discussion. Policymakers and their staff have very limited time and need materials that get the message across briefly and succinctly. The fact sheet should describe the issue you are raising, make the case for why policy change is needed to address it, and provide suggestions for how to solve the problem. Include an *ask*, that is, a request for action by the policymaker, whether it is to sign a letter, cosponsor a bill, introduce legislation, or attend an event in the district. Policymakers and their staff expect an ask from you that gives them an action item or goal that you want them to achieve as a result of the conversation. The action item is key because most members and staff want the meeting to be meaningful and know that their role is to help you.

Congressional staff work on a multitude of policy issues every day. A health care staffer, for example, might be working on malaria prevention, reimbursements for a particular drug in Medicare, disability issues, cancer treatment, and provisions in the Affordable Care Act all in one day. They experience an enormous amount of pressure to be as efficient and informed as possible. Making your talking points and materials easy to understand is a key component of having policy impact. The more accessible you can make your message, the more successful you will be. Think of it in terms of how you would explain your research to a stranger that you are sitting next to on a short bus ride. How would you describe the issue to someone who has no background in the topic whatsoever, and how would you make it relevant to that stranger in a short time? Meetings with congressional staff usually last no longer than 30 minutes. When preparing talking points and fact sheets, leave out details about research methods and statistics (e.g., effect sizes, confidence intervals, experimental designs) and focus instead on the issue that you want to discuss. Theoretical issues or arcane debates within the field are usually not important in the context of public policy. Keep the message to the policy issue at hand and how the research informs the issue.

Other ways of influencing policy include contributing to political campaigns and attending fundraisers for policymakers. This level of participation is not one that is usually pursued by academics and typically falls more within the realm of corporations, labor unions, large institutions, professional associations, and other interest groups, including nonprofit leaders. This tactic may even seem anathema to some; however, it is important to mention it as an effective tactic. The APA Practice Organization Political Action Committee (APAPO-PAC), for example, works to support House and Senate candidates who are "friends of psychology." The APAPO-PAC "focuses intensely on addressing practitioners' and educators' concerns, such as reimbursement for psychological services, inappropriate barriers to psychologists' scope of practice and funding for psychology education" ("About Psychology PAC," n.d.). Many other professional associations employ this tactic extensively. For example, health providers (e.g., medical associations) regularly host fundraisers for members of Congress to put the spotlight on issues of importance to them. The truth of the matter is, policymakers have to raise money to fund their campaigns, and this is one of the ways that they do so. One of the reasons that the Tea Party has been so successful is because it understood this method for influencing policymakers. By putting up and funding candidates that represent their perspective, the Tea Party has been successful at toppling some of the longest-standing and most powerful members of Congress.

Another way to influence policy at the federal level is by lobbying and developing relationships with officials in federal agencies who are responsible for implementing the laws that Congress enacts. You can also lobby the White House directly, usually as part of a national coalition on an issue. Engaging the executive branch by submitting comments on federal rulemaking or participating in federal conferences is also effective in influencing federal policy outcomes.

CONCLUSION

Psychology has an enormous amount to offer public policy. Yet, our field has a long way to go to become more effective at disseminating our research and encouraging participation in relevant policy debates. Rather than looking at policy participation as an optional side interest of psychologists, academic institutions should instead recognize the value of disseminating our research beyond the academy to the policy realm and incentivize this form of engagement. Our field needs structural change in the way that it trains students and rewards how research is communicated to the power structure of our country. There should be tangible professional rewards for speaking at congressional briefings, testifying at hearings, and becoming a known and influential resource for policymakers.

In a recent article in *American Psychologist* about "public perceptions of psychology," psychologist Christopher Ferguson (2015) argued that self-inflicted "internal problems" within psychological science have "limited its impact with policymakers, other scientists, and the public" (p. 1). Ferguson blamed APA's "overuse of politicized policy statements" (p. 1) as part of the "problem" and stated that "it is unlikely that either organizations such as the

APA or individual scholars are likely to be successful at operating as both scientists and advocates at the same time" (p. 7). This perspective, published in one of the premier journals of the APA, dismisses the value of psychologists influencing policy. This kind of viewpoint limits psychology's reach. There is no reason why scientific objectivity should conflict with advocacy. Sharing rigorous research findings with policymakers is a practical application of our field and does not diminish the scientific soundness of our research. Rather than suggest that it is problematic for psychologists and our premier trade association to engage in influencing policy, I would argue that it is our responsibility to engage in public policy. When we have undertaken important and relevant research, we should do as much as possible to engage in policy debates and put our research to use in pragmatic ways. There is too much at stake to remain on the sidelines.

And let's consider for a moment the alternative: If we do not speak up and put forth the effort to share our research with policymakers, other more engaged citizens and organizations will frame and inform the debates for us. Whether we like it or not, the loudest and most consistently heard voices will shape the future of our country; it would be a travesty to let ideological groups that ignore empirical research continue to shape policy agendas based on the volume of their voices rather than the substance of their argument—especially given the extensive and rigorously tested scientific knowledge that we have generated through our scholarship.

Psychologists have the privilege of doctoral degrees, a high level of education and training, and the prestige that comes with academic appointments at universities and other institutions. That privilege and those advantages should be put to use more extensively in the policy realm. Other groups have developed the means for influencing policy through hard work, persistence, and using the system to their advantage, without any scientific background or training to back up their positions. Psychologists, on the other hand, are in a unique position as professionals in a field that has generated empirical research on a very broad range of issues. We need to do more to put our knowledge and insights to work to make the world a better place with research as the platform that informs our positions and furthers our reach.

REFERENCES

About Psychology PAC. (n.d.). Retrieved from http://www.supportpsychologypac. org/about.aspx

Ferguson, C. J. (2015). "Everybody knows psychology is not a real science": Public perceptions of psychology and how we can improve our relationship with policymakers, the scientific community, and the general public. *American Psychologist, 70*, 527–542. http://dx.doi.org/10.1037/a0039405

5

Government and Organizations: Transforming Institutions Using Behavioral Insights

Abigail Dalton and Max H. Bazerman

It is only in the past few years that we have observed a massive acceleration in the demand for ideas from psychology to improve outcomes in governments across the globe. Since the publication of *Nudge* (Thaler & Sunstein, 2008) and *Thinking, Fast and Slow* (Kahneman, 2011), public attention to and knowledge of behavioral science have been augmented by the success of its applications in the field and the remarkable potential for a multitude of policy applications. Here, we describe how we got here and what psychologists can do to increase the impact of their research in government and organizations.

Any history on the role of psychology in public policy is bound to be influenced by the background of the writers, and we are not exempt. Dalton has been the assistant director of the Behavioral Insights Group (BIG) at Harvard University since 2013. Bazerman has been in the behavioral decision

http://dx.doi.org/10.1037/0000066-006
Making Research Matter: A Psychologist's Guide to Public Engagement, L. R. Tropp (Editor)
Copyright © 2018 by the American Psychological Association. All rights reserved.

research world for decades and received his doctorate from Carnegie Mellon University (CMU). Herbert Simon's Nobel Prize–winning work on bounded rationality (March & Simon, 1958; Simon & Barnard, 1947), which argues that humans were bounded in their rationality, was part of the intellectual fabric of CMU. Years later, Tversky and Kahneman (1974; Kahneman & Tversky 1979) created the modern field of behavioral decision research by delineating the systematic and predictable ways in which individuals deviated from rational decision making. This research led to fascinating lab experiments that showed surprising mistakes that are made by even the best and the brightest, and these effects have proven very robust, with excellent track records at generalizing to field contexts. Early scholars in this field clearly had the idea that if they understood their intuitive departures from rationality, they could then eliminate these errors. However, decades of research found that although researchers were great at identifying what humans did wrong, they had minimal ability to create permanent improvements in their intuitive decision making (Bazerman & Moore, 2013).

CAN BEHAVIORAL SCIENCE REALLY MAKE A DIFFERENCE?

A critical turning point was the 2008 publication of *Nudge* by Thaler (a behavioral economist) and Sunstein (a legal scholar), who were both deeply connected to the work of psychologists such as Kahneman, Tversky, and Cialdini. The basic idea of *Nudge* is that even though researchers do not know much about how to fix intuition, they can understand it well enough to redesign the choice architecture that affects decisions so that wiser decisions will result. A classic example of this idea comes from Thaler's earlier work on *Save More Tomorrow*, which encourages workers to commit to increasing their savings rates in advance of a pay increase and continue to do so until a preset maximum. The employee can opt out at any time, but they are making decisions with their future selves in mind and not when confronted with what feels like a windfall. The results were dramatic, with a threefold increase in saving.

By combining knowledge from psychology, economics, and other related areas, researchers are better able to understand the driving factors behind human behavior and decision making. Acknowledging the psychological limits of human rationality consequently enables researchers to determine how to better influence human behavior, and this research can have tremendous implications for policy. *Nudge* is rife with such examples: Moving healthy lunchtime options into accessible areas—and unhealthy options out of sight—increases the likelihood that consumers will select healthier meal options; defaulting citizens into organ donation dramatically increases donation rates overall; lowering credit card rates encourages slower rates of repayment; and having complicated websites, like those for Medicare and Medicaid, makes it virtually impossible for people to make informed and simple decisions. In each of these instances, insights from human psychology have had tremendous impact on policies and entire populations.

One need only look to the success of international entities engaged in this work to see tangible results from implementing psychology ideas in policy—most notably, the Behavioural Insights Team (BIT) in the United Kingdom, which has led numerous policy changes founded in behavioral science research to great economic and popular success. Working with the Cabinet Office in 2010, David Halpern, BIT's director, began looking to create big wins in the policy space with uncontroversial early trials. Their earliest experiments involved changing the wording of letters that went out to citizens with delinquent tax records, to great success. As reported by *The Independent*,

> One experiment involved Her Majesty's Revenue and Customs (HMRC) secretly changing the wording of tens of thousands of tax letters, leading to the collection of an extra £200m in income tax. . . . "The normal repayment rate is about 50 per cent. The [new] letter says: '94 per cent of people pay their tax on time', so now you emphasis [sic] the underlying social norm—and then: 'Even if one person doesn't it has a significant impact.' The repayment rate went up to 85 per cent, [collecting] £200m just in that experiment." ("Nudge, nudge, wink wink," 2011)

Key to the successful growth of behavioral science in policy is looking for easy, economically and politically uncontroversial early wins. BIT recognized this when they began with tax nudging and have shepherded that success into other more interesting and socially impactful areas, including education, employment, and health. As we write this chapter, BIT has completed more than 200 field experiments, all aimed at using psychological thought and field experimentation to demonstrate better ways to run the government. They have improved school attendance, improved diversity recruitment in police forces, reduced no-shows to medical appointments, and more.

Little else can so nicely illustrate the extraordinary and growing interest in the field of behavioral science and policy than the presence of nearly a thousand people in a single conference space, eagerly listening to dozens of speakers as they outline the numerous applications of this work. Shortly before preparing this chapter, we returned from a conference in London entitled "BX2015," or Behavioural Exchange 2015, organized by BIT (the Nudge Unit). Most of the 2-day conference was about how an understanding of psychology could be used to transform the functioning of government in domains that included increasing organ donations, increasing school attendance rates, raising tax revenues, and improving compliance with health care recommendations, among a host of other worthy applications. In attendance were academics, consultants, grant makers, and primarily public-sector policymakers. This conference is part of a powerful movement to use behavioral insights to make governments and other organizations more effective, and it is changing the degree to which the real world not only knows about psychological insights but also uses those insights to transform how government works.

THE BEHAVIORAL INSIGHTS GROUP AT HARVARD

Many other countries and entities are actively forming nudge units, and consulting firms and funding agencies are actively exploring their role in this new field (and were well represented at the London conference). Sound social policy research should be based on high-quality basic research, and collaboration with academics is essential. At Harvard University, the presence of a critical mass of behavioral scientists has led to the emergence of BIG, an entity aimed at connecting academics to emerging government nudge units, with the goal of training students in the field. Launched in 2013 by cochairs Max Bazerman and Iris Bohnet, BIG, under the auspices of the Harvard Kennedy School's Center for Public Leadership, integrates Harvard's outstanding collection of scholars who use behavioral insights through field experiments for the public good. This group involves an active collaboration of scholars from Harvard Business School, Harvard Kennedy School, Harvard Law School, Harvard Medical School, Harvard Graduate School of Education, Harvard School of Public Health, and the government and economics departments within the Faculty of Arts and Sciences.

Though BIG began as an entity with a primary goal of increasing faculty collaboration, we have found immense demand from governments and organizations for training and collaborative opportunities—and with good reason. For leaders, insights from academia can lead directly to impactful policy change. BIG plays a central role in helping leaders create environments that promote more ethical and evidence-based decision making, advance the well-being of society, increase voter turnout, create better educational systems, reduce discrimination, protect the environment, improve financial decisions, diminish societal risks, and ameliorate health—all by helping individuals, groups, organizations, and society make better decisions. Our faculty focus their attention on varied fields; for instance, Francesca Gino and Leslie John work to find ways to reduce institutional and individual cheating; Todd Rogers aims to improve student outcomes by increasing parental involvement; John Beshears, David Laibson, and Brigitte Madrian work to increase employee uptake of savings vehicles; and Jim Greiner works with legal aid clinics to find the most effective methods of applying behavioral science practices to law to best allocate limited resources for optimal legal outcomes for victims.

BIG's faculty recognize that their research can have tremendous impact in the public sector, and we leverage our connections to international entities to that purpose. By partnering with governments that are doing this work—including BIT in the United Kingdom and emerging units in Singapore, Australia, Israel, and the Netherlands, among others, many of whom have been inspired (and advised) by BIT—BIG works to provide opportunities to policymakers, present and future, to apply these insights to the real world. As more organizations realize the power of applying behavioral science to policy and governments take up this work—including the White House Office of Science and Technology's Social and Behavioral Sciences Team, developed under the Obama administration, which in 2015 released a report outlining how behavioral science can improve outcomes for government agencies and constituents—practitioners would do well to learn from this growing and fascinating field.

Soon after we started BIG in 2013, our faculty membership included more than 30 faculty affiliates, all of whom used behavioral insights to devise field experiments for the public good (see http://cpl.hks.harvard.edu/behavioral-insights-group for details). Professional school students also started to show up in large numbers asking about the kinds of roles they could play in BIG. We were clearly surprised. We had no idea that this level of applied student interest existed. A loose coalition of interested students soon formed and began organizing lunch sessions with BIG faculty. The Behavioral Insights Study Group (or BISG, as it is known) holds weekly sessions with academics and professionals, holds workshops and career panels with organizations, and disseminates a weekly newsletter to more than 600 members. Crucially, BISG is a great example of how harnessing interested students can prepare them to enter a variety of fields where they might apply behavioral science to policy.

HOW SHOULD RESEARCHERS APPROACH WORKING WITH GOVERNMENT AND ORGANIZATIONS?

Through the classes we offer, we have been able to provide students with the opportunity to work with clients seeking genuine solutions to agency problems by using psychological insights. Students quickly learn that, effective as these applications are, applying them to different cultural and organizational contexts comes with its own challenges, and they learn a few guiding principles and useful insights as they engage in this work.

Know Your Clients

Students find that their challenges differ somewhat depending on the goals and starting knowledge of the clients with whom they work. For students working with clients who already have an existing and nuanced understanding of behavioral research, the primary challenge is coming up with novel and potentially effective solutions beyond what the clients had already considered. For students working with clients who are considerably less familiar with behavioral research, the primary challenge is explaining the importance and effectiveness of experiments that might support proposed changes.

Experiments are crucial—and often, game-changing—elements of demonstrating the power of behavioral insights. Organizations, however, can be wary of using them to test out ideas prior to implementation. For example, after one of our student groups presented a proposal to their client concerning signage around waste disposal in the Netherlands, the client was so enthusiastic that they were eager to proceed toward implementation without experimental trials. Emphasizing the importance of experimental trials to demonstrate what works and what doesn't work will make later experimental testing and implementation easier. In this particular case, Bazerman explained to the client that even an experiment in which 90% of participants receive the experimental message—and 10% do not—can firmly prove the effectiveness of the change in message, without eliminating the potential for widespread impact. Other organizations may simply be wary of any kind of experimentation or testing; with such opposition, beginning with a low-cost, economically appealing initiative that saves the organization money may prove the effectiveness of behavioral insights and enable later trials and policy changes.

Expect Reluctance to Change

Generally, students encountered a reluctance to change what had been in place for years. It is essential to emphasize that just because something has always been done in a particular way does not mean it always should remain intractably the same. Things such as forms, rules, and policies were all created by individuals with the same biases and shortsightedness that all human beings suffer from. But by taking what we know from field and lab research, we can test and implement effective changes.

Start Small

Relatedly, students also found that small but powerful changes were more likely to be embraced and applied by their clients. Therefore, when we engage with organizations and governments, we emphasize the ways in which significant change can be made through even small adaptations and low-cost implementation (e.g., moving a signature line on a form). For example, if you want people to fill out a form (e.g., a tax return) honestly, does it make more sense to

(a) have people fill out a form and sign it after completing the form to note that the information is accurate, or

(b) sign a statement before filling out the form agreeing that the information that they are about to provide is true?

Shu, Mazar, Gino, Ariely, and Bazerman (2012) have shown that *b* is far more effective than *a*, reducing dishonesty in the lab by about 50%. Moreover, Shu et al. used and cited a great deal of social psychology to develop this prediction. Furthermore, in our experience, if you ask academics or nonacademic practitioners this question, the vast majority come up with this same answer. The amazing fact is that governments across the globe have gotten this wrong for decades.

From studies like these to examples of students working with clients, we find that simple changes can often have the greatest impact. And because such changes are small and easy to implement, they are more likely to be adopted. Individuals looking to apply behavioral science to policy in their own organizations should similarly focus on the attainable, starting small and simple. Academia provides numerous examples of worthwhile changes to policy to improve outcomes for organizations and society. But proceed with care, and consider what is possible (and likely to succeed) within your particular context.

ARE PSYCHOLOGISTS RECEIVING CREDIT FOR BEHAVIORAL INSIGHTS?

As the behavioral insights movement has developed, behavioral economics has often been recognized as the field at the core of the ideas. Psychologists have been quick to (correctly) note that many behavioral economics insights are straightforward applications of ideas that were published in psychology decades before. Understandably, then, psychologists may be miffed by the misdirected credit for their work, given that most of the work of behavioral economists is firmly rooted in much earlier work by psychologists. Economists frequently provide limited citations for the actual root of their ideas. And the ideas that often go under the popular label of behavioral economics are often fairly basic psychology. Economists have also noted that the United States has a Council of Economic Advisers and no Council of Psychological Advisers, and many psychologists have questioned the wisdom of that situation.

We believe that psychologists have a right to be annoyed when they are not credited fully for their contribution to idea generation. At the same time, as we pursue the goal of making the world a better place through transforming government and organizations, we believe it would be useful for academic psychologists to identify changes in their own behavior to get their due credit and to get their ideas implemented most effectively. Moreover, we believe that psychologists are uniquely placed to enact change; through their insights, individuals looking to implement policy change through the utilization of behavioral science are able to look to both academia and other governments to determine how best to move forward. For us, the critical questions are why psychologists have had limited direct impact and how to change this moving forward.

Lab Research Versus Field Research

As psychologists, we have a long tradition of doing most of our research in well-controlled laboratory settings. Economics research has much more commonly been conducted in field settings. Pure field experiments were fairly rare across both fields as of a decade ago, but they have caught on. Some use the terms *randomized controlled trials* (most commonly in behavioral research), *A/B testing* (most commonly in high tech), or *clinical trials* (in pharmaceutical contexts) to refer to these kinds of studies. However, all basically test some novel strategy (in a treatment condition) against the way the world works without that strategy (in a control condition). The good news is that the vast majority of the important research findings discovered by psychologists in laboratory settings that have later been tested in the field hold up amazingly well. However, government and organizational leaders continue to want field experiments showing the same effect to be convinced to implement the proposed change. For example, laboratory studies by Shu et al. (2012) showing that people are more honest in reporting when first signing a form did not get the attention of governments. However, when these researchers added a field experiment showing how an insurance company used this strategy to improve honesty in odometer readings (which affect your car insurance premium), their ability to interest government grew dramatically. The U.S. government has similarly shown the strategy to be effective in fee payment, and BIT has initial evidence on tax collection in a developing economy.

As a lab experimenter, Bazerman is coming to grips with the descriptive fact that policymakers are more convinced by simple field evidence than by evidence from labs—despite the excellent track record of lab experiments and that he has done the vast majority of his empirical work in labs. And behavioral economists have adapted to this descriptive fact much faster than have psychologists. Perhaps this situation is acceptable, given that psychological ideas are being implemented. However, ignoring the real-world preference for field experiments is a limitation that can affect psychologists' ability to play a more direct role as the behavioral insight movement evolves.

Novelty Versus Impact

It is also important to note a tension between researchers in nudge units and basic academics. Typically, academics are, and are trained to be, in love with their newest idea. In contrast, nudge units want to know what works. They are unlikely to care about how new the effect is, instead being far more interested in how it can be used—such as to collect taxes, educate children, or make citizens healthier. There is no magic answer to resolve these different preferences, but ignoring them is unlikely to be the best answer. Psychologists who want to have their ideas implemented therefore need to think about how their (typically lab-based) research evidence can be used to create opportunities for initial field demonstrations as a lever to greater access.

Significance Versus Size of Effect

For many researchers, finding a significant effect has been a critical goal in the scientific process. However, lab researchers have typically not been too concerned about the size of the effect, and for good reason—in the lab, the size of the effect can be influenced by the nature of the manipulation and research procedures used. In contrast, policymakers are much more interested in the size of the effect. They want to know how much your intervention can add to taxes collected, students showing up for school, or people showing up for doctor's appointments. Economists have had an advantage in this arena, as their history of working with field data has always led them to focus on interpreting the beta coefficient from the regression equation. Lab-based psychologists have been largely out of sync in the dialogue, and those psychologists who are able to adapt to applied goals are likely to be more effective in connecting to change makers.

Time in Academia Versus Government

Imagine that you heard that your tenure-track colleague was taking 2 years off to go work in Washington. To most psychologists, this is a strange career move. Psychologists have rarely viewed time out of academia as a good thing. In contrast, economists have a long history of treating leaves to join the government as an acceptable career path, and they are welcomed back to academia after their stint in government. Both the actual acceptability of such a leave and, more broadly, the mentality that there are things to learn in government create an environment in which economists are positioned to have greater impact.

CONCLUSION

At BIG, we have been fortunate to have a rich academic and curricular setting to encourage the interest of our students and enable the research and collaborative opportunities of our faculty as the behavioral science research and practice space grow. But academics and students need not feel limited in their efforts if they do not have a behavioral science–specific research or government entity of their own. To play a role in this new movement, knowing the basics is essential. We expect all our students to read *Nudge* and *Thinking, Fast and Slow* before they enter the classroom to gain a base-level of knowledge in the field. The growing interest in the field may also provide useful templates and examples for those looking to apply these insights in their own countries or organizations. Emerging nudge units and behavioral science departments within governments and organizations worldwide, as well as the research done by behavioral scientists at Harvard and elsewhere, offer copious examples from which to draw. Look for examples of policy changes and trials that have worked in cultural contexts similar to your own, and determine whether they are applicable in your particular context.

REFERENCES

Bazerman, M. H., & Moore, D. A. (2013). *Judgment in managerial decision making*. Hoboken, NJ: Wiley.

Kahneman, D. (2011). *Thinking, fast and slow*. New York, NY: Farrar, Straus and Giroux.

Kahneman, D., & Tversky, A. (1979). Prospect theory: An analysis of decision under risk. *Econometrica, 47*, 263–292.

March, J. G., & Simon, H. A. (1958). *Organizations*. New York, NY: Wiley.

Nudge, nudge, wink wink . . . How the government wants to change the way we think. (2011, January 3). *The Independent*. Retrieved from http://www.

independent.co.uk/news/uk/politics/nudge-nudge-wink-wink-how-the-government-wants-to-change-the-way-we-think-2174655.html

Shu, L., Mazar, N., Gino, F., Ariely, D., & Bazerman, M. (2012). Signing at the beginning makes ethics salient and decreases dishonest self-reports in comparison to signing at the end. *Proceedings of the National Academy of Sciences, 109,* 15197–15200.

Simon, H. A., & Barnard, C. I. (1947). *Administrative behavior: A study of decision-making processes in administrative organization.* New York, NY: Macmillan.

Thaler, R. H., & Sunstein, C. R. (2008). *Nudge: Improving decisions about health, wealth, and happiness.* New Haven, CT: Yale University Press.

Tversky, A., & Kahneman, D. (1974). Judgment under uncertainty: Heuristics and biases. *Science, 185,* 1124–1131. http://dx.doi.org/10.1126/science.185.4157.1124

6

The Courts: How to Translate Research for Legal Cases

Eugene Borgida and Susan T. Fiske

Suppose you are in your office one morning, peacefully preparing for class, and your phone rings. You reluctantly answer, and at the other end of the call is an employment-discrimination lawyer who has read some of your research on stereotyping, prejudice, and discrimination and claims that some of your colleagues recommended you. She wants to know if you would be interested in serving as an expert witness in her client's discrimination lawsuit.

Appropriately, you ask the lawyer to tell you more about the case. (Just to make this more real, we are using an actual case as a hypothetical; see Blount, 2015a, 2015b.) Since 1998, the lawyer explains, her client, Shannon Miller, had been the women's ice hockey coach at the University of Minnesota Duluth (UMD). She was not only the highest paid women's hockey coach in the United States but unquestionably one of the most successful. Yet in December 2014, Miller's coaching contract at UMD was not renewed.

http://dx.doi.org/10.1037/0000066-007
Making Research Matter: A Psychologist's Guide to Public Engagement, L. R. Tropp (Editor)
Copyright © 2018 by the American Psychological Association. All rights reserved.

The university said that the decision was difficult but claimed it could no longer afford Miller's base salary. So, Miller sought legal representation and has now filed a lawsuit against UMD claiming discrimination based on gender, sexual orientation (Miller is openly gay), age, and national origin (Miller is a Canadian as well as U.S. citizen). In addition, Miller claims that UMD created a hostile work environment, retaliated against her and other female coaches, violated equal pay laws, and violated Title IX of the U.S. Education Amendments of 1972 enforced by the Department of Education's Office of Civil Rights. The lawyer also dutifully informs you that UMD denied that the school discriminated against her client, and they expressed confidence that the claims would be refuted in court.

WHAT DOES AN ACADEMIC LIKE ME HAVE TO OFFER TO LITIGATORS?

At this point you are feeling overwhelmed, wondering, "Why the heck did I ever pick up the phone? What role can I play in such litigation, as I have never served as an expert in a legal case? What exactly are they asking me to do, and am I qualified to do it?"

Over the years, both of us have asked ourselves the same questions on numerous occasions. For Fiske, for example, it all started with a phone call as in the Miller case (with lawyers, it's usually a phone call—no paper trail). Would she testify in a gender discrimination case in employment, apparently the first to use behavioral science expert testimony, parallel to *Brown v. Board of Education of Topeka*'s (1954) historic use of social science in a race discrimination case? How could Fiske say no, if she believed our research to be useful? She said yes, educated herself about her legal role, read boxes of evidence, prepared the heck out of her testimony, suffered through an obnoxious deposition, and became increasingly nervous as the trial approached, only to learn that the case settled the night before the trial. The attorneys were kind enough to say that her presence helped leverage a good outcome for the plaintiff, but for Fiske as a would-be expert, it was a bittersweet anticlimax. Lesson #1: Most cases settle. Sometimes just being ready to testify is enough. And other times, cases go forward, survive multiple appeals, and appear in textbooks (*Hopkins v. Price Waterhouse*, 1985). You never know.

Borgida has fielded similar calls inquiring about expert witness testimony in single-plaintiff and class action discrimination cases as well as opportunities to present research at law school conferences or colloquia; to advise the Equal Employment Opportunity Commission (EEOC); to write a law review article; and to collaborate with others on an amicus brief. It turns out, as we highlight in this chapter, academics have multiple roles to play in the legal arena. Our focus in this chapter, however, is on the expert witness role, as this is one that psychologists often encounter and the one that we have played most frequently over our careers. The expert witness role has effectively transported a wide range of psychological science to the courts, from research on children as witnesses (Ceci & Bruck, 2006) to research on eyewitness identification (Wells, 2016) and false confessions (Kassin, 2015).

WHAT WILL LITIGATORS MOST WANT FROM ME?

So let's return to your phone call from the attorney in the discrimination case involving Shannon Miller, the aforementioned UMD women's ice hockey coach. Recall that the attorney contacted you after being given your name by some colleagues who were familiar with your research on stereotyping, prejudice, and discrimination. After you learn about the case from the attorney during this initial phone call, what is your next step? Before you make your decision to participate or not, it is always wise to ask the attorney to send the complaint and any other pertinent case material (e.g., affidavits, deposition transcripts, EEOC rulings). This material is crucial to you being able to determine whether your relevant psychological expertise is likely to provide a sound, scientific context for understanding the case facts. You are essentially being asked to serve as an "honest broker" of science (Eagly, 2016), an expert whose research background and bona fides will enable you to "communicate consensus scientific findings . . . in an effort to encourage exploration of evidence-based . . . options" (p. 199).

You must take this step before agreeing to serve as an expert witness because the trial judge will be serving as the scientific gatekeeper, committed to keeping out junk science, as required by *Daubert v. Merrell Dow Pharmaceuticals* (1993) and its heirs (i.e., *General Electric Co. v. Joiner*, 1997, and *Kumho Tire Co., Ltd. v. Carmichael*, 1999). The judge will particularly want to know if the science on prejudice, stereotyping, and discrimination that you are qualified to offer on Shannon Miller's behalf as an expert witness is reliable and relevant to the case facts and meets the requirements of Federal Rule of Evidence 702:

> A witness who is qualified as an expert by knowledge, skill, experience, training, or education may testify in the form of an opinion or otherwise if: (a) The expert's scientific, technical, or other specialized knowledge will help the trier of fact to understand the evidence or to determine a fact in issue; (b) The testimony is based on sufficient facts or data; (c) The testimony is the product of reliable principles and methods; and (d) The expert has reliably applied the principles and methods to the facts of the case. (United States Code, 2015, p. 387)

In other words, the focus for the judge will be on the scientific standing and integrity of the science at hand.

If you judge that, after a review of the legal material you requested, sound peer-reviewed science will enable you to be an honest broker of science relevant to the case facts, then by all means you ought to consider serving as an expert witness in the case. But before you officially agree to serve, make sure that you ask the attorney for as much of the case material as possible to review, including all depositions and exhibits (note that it is not unusual to be asked to sign a confidentiality agreement that prohibits you from discussing the case outside of the litigation context). Make this request comprehensive so that you avoid being the recipient of a biased sampling of the case materials. Being given a selective subset of case materials necessarily exposes you to the criticism by opposing counsel that your science-based perspective on the case facts was skewed by the plaintiff attorney's selectivity and that your expert views are therefore tainted by a confirmatory bias rather than reflecting a balanced view of the case facts. However, because the attorney may be reluctant to pay for your review of all the relevant documentation without your agreement to testify, you may either (a) request a specific subset that you select a priori, (b) randomly sample from the case files, or (c) review the material on spec with the agreement of pay if you decide to testify. Each method has its advantages and disadvantages, but the goal is the same: to remain as objective as possible for this case and to protect your reputation generally.

As in our hypothetical expert witness inquiry in the Shannon Miller case, attorneys who are considering experts for their cases will find you based on referrals and networking and, more important, on the basis of your published scientific work and its perceived pertinence to their case. Your research track record and skill set, not the luster of your LinkedIn site, will best position you to consider an expert witness opportunity. But as we discuss in the remainder of this chapter, how you present your science, especially to nonacademic audiences, has emerged as a crucial factor in presenting psychological science in the legal arena.

HOW CAN I COMMUNICATE SCIENTIFIC INFORMATION EFFECTIVELY TO LITIGATORS AND THE COURTS?

Clear communication is clear communication, everywhere, but our role as exporters of our science has some special caveats distinctive to the legal context.

Write What You Know

Authors learn that writing what they know is the first rule of honest writing. So, too, do psychological scientists communicating to legal audiences. Operationally, this means agreeing to not communicate outside your areas of legitimate expertise—demonstrated by what you know, what you can show that you know, and what you do not know by virtue of your training, publications, teaching, editing, consulting, and previous testimony. Don't be tempted to stretch your claims to expertise in response to what you or the legal client may wish you could claim with authority. Do be confident in what you legitimately know; after all, it's what you do for a living, and it goes beyond common sense (Borgida & Fiske, 2008).

Write What the Field Knows

Science is always incomplete, a work in progress (or else it wouldn't be science). Nevertheless, we know some things with more confidence than we know others. Scientific experts operate under the precedent set by *Daubert v. Merrell Dow Pharmaceuticals* (1993) and its heirs. One of *Daubert*'s criteria is that evidence introduced by an expert must be reliable and scientifically valid and acceptable in the pertinent scientific community. So, remember that you must represent the generally accepted evidence-based viewpoint, not just your own renegade minority opinion, however convincing to you personally. Conveying quality science must represent not only consensus but also peer-reviewed consensus (Fiske & Borgida, 2011a). Exemplars of foundational sources include National Academy of Sciences consensus-study reports, journals published by *Annual Reviews, Psychological Bulletin* (its reviews are often meta-analyses), *Psychological Science in the Public Interest*, and *Policy Insights From the Behavioral and Brain Sciences*. All of these undergo peer review, which adds to their credibility.

Be an Honest Broker

Our credibility as experts lies in our being competent (credentialed) and trustworthy (honest) communicators. One rule is to not let the adversarial setting shape your message. Don't take the case if social science is not relevant; make sure that you think you have useful science to offer. Don't take the case if it's dubious; sometimes attorneys think we are a magic bullet, but we can't salvage a weak case. Don't stretch the evidence to suit your side; what you are asked to opine on depends, of course, on who retains you. That should determine the focus of what you can and should say. Beyond that, follow the Gricean rules of communication (Grice, 1975): Be truthful, informative, relevant, complete, and concise—in short, cooperative—but you are not required to help the other side. They most likely will have their own expert who is being paid to scrutinize and then rebut the science you present.

Be Direct

Say something as conclusive as honestly possible. Don't talk like a scholar: Don't obfuscate. Consistent with being an honest broker but also a clear communicator, don't unnecessarily hedge, qualify, equivocate. If you can't make any judgments about the case at hand, what are you doing there? Draw warranted conclusions, but avoid exaggerated causal claims. Remember that, at the end of the day, preserving your own credibility and integrity, and that of the science you offer, matters the most.

Be Clear

Once during a break in her testimony, Fiske overheard one of the judge's law clerks exclaim to the other: "Psych 101!" Removing herself from overhearing any more, she endeavored to make her postbreak testimony less academic and more straightforwardly to the point, in case they felt it was a tiresome elementary lecture. Although we may find psychology fascinating in its own right, the court wants to know what the expert offers, not pass a graduate qualifying exam or even an intro psych exam. Get to the point, with as little jargon as possible, and get out.

Be Trustworthy

Fortunately, too, your testimony indeed is trustworthy, or else you would not be offering it. Social psychologists know that, to be persuasive, communicators must be expert (as noted) and trustworthy. The public— and doubtless the court—basically respects scientists' expertise, but a scientist's trustworthiness has to be established (Fiske & Dupree, 2014). Chances are you will not be challenged on the basis of your credentials or qualifications, but rest assured that an effort nevertheless might be made to exclude you—such as proposing mercenary or ideological motives for your agreeing to consult in the first place; do not take it personally.

Be Firm

If you are not confident in your conclusions, no one else will be. Decide in private what you can say in public, and then speak firmly. Certainly, share any doubts with the counsel who has retained you, but resist pressure even from your side to smooth over rough edges or go beyond the data for the sake of sharper advocacy. The adversarial context will eat you alive if you are too uncertain, too nice, or too informal.

Keep in mind that the audience who matters—whose trust and respect an expert must gain—is not the opposing attorney, who is paid to remain skeptical. The audience isn't even the client, who does not have to like what you say, as long as it represents the science. Instead, the main audience is the trier of fact, the judge or jury, who will decide the case.

WHAT ELSE CAN I EXPECT AS AN EXPERT WITNESS?

For a psychological scientist seeking to provide insights in legal settings, the most salient culture clash is the tension between the pressures of an adversarial legal context and rigorous scientific integrity. Like any culture, its customs can be learned, and the visit can be rewarding. But, as our experience has shown, knowing what to expect and being prepared is crucial.

Expect No Mercy

No one will give you the benefit of the doubt. You are not among friends, except for the attorney who retained you. A few tactics may be novel, compared with academic culture: They may ask how much you are being paid, whether you've ever testified for the other side, whether the retaining attorneys modified your testimony, and whether you belong to a political organization sympathetic to your client's plight. They can even demand all your e-mail exchanges with the attorney or colleagues concerning the case and all of your notes and annotations in the margins of the documents you have reviewed. We have confronted all these questions and more. One of us had a cross-examiner threaten to subpoena her computer's hard drive. Their message: "Professor X, do you really expect the court to buy that hokum?" Fortunately, it is the job of your client's attorney to object to inappropriate attacks and to resurrect your credibility afterward.

Expect Attacks

Imagine a hostile, well-informed colloquium audience, who have conspired beforehand to play "kill the speaker." Or imagine your most hostile reviewers. These examples convey some of the experience of being deposed by the opposing attorney, reading the opposing expert's rebuttal report, or being cross-examined. The opponents will do their best to destroy your testimony, seeking to expose weakness, express disbelief, convey contempt, provoke you, impugn your motives, and derogate your scientific training. Anticipate the counterarguments. Expert testimony can be a verbal chess game, so it pays to predict the opponent's likely strategy and guard against it. Admit to salient, significant controversies and weaknesses, counterarguing them in advance. Most good journal articles own up to limitations but explain why they don't undermine the main message. Use your judgment here.

Expect the Unexpected: Document, Document, Document

One of us once headed off a hostile cross-examination by bringing to court several feet of deposition transcript binders, their pages marked with a couple hundred sticky notes. What that did was force the cross-examining attorney to choose between challenging every bit of evidence and avoiding a litany of examples unfavorable to their case. In the same way, you should document sources for your expert report as would a paranoid intellectual with advanced obsessive–compulsive disorder. Every sentence should have a footnote with a specific page number and a phrase summarizing the reference's relevance. Assume a junior law-firm associate will check every citation, hoping to find a "gotcha." Overwhelm them with pertinent references, and not just to your own publications, because you have to establish consensus.

Conclusions on Expert Witnessing

Our advice concerning communication applies directly to oral expert testimony, a late step in a complex process. Prior to that will likely occur exploratory contacts, retainer arrangements, discovery of evidence, a written report, a deposition taken by the opposition, and strategic phone conversations or meetings with the retaining attorneys. The logistics are not trivial, and they are unfamiliar but knowable (e.g., being aware of the importance of paper trails). Our main advice is to consider carefully what case(s) you accept, knowing that lawyers will want everything from you yesterday and they may press you to say what you cannot. Nevertheless, expert witnessing has been some of the most exciting, challenging, rewarding, and stimulating work we have ever done.

WHAT OTHER ROLES MIGHT I PLAY IN THE LEGAL REALM?

Engagement in the legal arena, as we have suggested, involves multiple roles and not just the expert witness role. You might consider a broader range of venues for psychological science serving the legal context, including amicus briefs, law review articles, speeches, applicable research, contract research, and engagement through other legal channels.

Amicus Briefs

Most commonly found in cases before the U.S. Supreme Court, amicus curiae ("friend of the court") briefs often result from an organization with a perspective to offer (e.g., the American Psychological Association [APA], other professional societies, policy advocacy organizations). As such, amicus briefs are typically written by committee. They are essentially literature reviews that inform the court and take a position on the case accordingly. Psychologists are often called upon not only to be signatories on these briefs but to assist litigators and policy advocates in identifying the most relevant aspects of the research literature and to review the sections of the briefs relevant to their expertise, to ensure that the scientific research has been reported accurately.

Law Review Articles

Law review articles, especially those that fall under the rubric of empirical legal scholarship, also are literature reviews; however, they tend to focus on the relevance of existing science to a broad legal issue, rather than on a specific case. Some social scientists have strategically placed their work in law reviews, rather than psychology journals, to maximize exposure of their ideas to the legal community (Fiske & Borgida, 2011b).

Unlike with articles submitted to psychology journals, you can submit a law review manuscript to several journals at once, but then you must take the first acceptance and decline the rest. Sometimes, articles are invited by a specific journal. In all cases, the editors are law students, who make the final decision and who edit compulsively. If the law review article presents empirical research, then chances are the student law editor assigned to the paper will seek outside expertise on the science, as a proxy for peer review. This student-led editing process has pros and cons, but it puts a premium on documentation and clarity. Alternatively, if your research connects with legal and policy issues, then you might try to publish some of your work in journals at the intersection of psychological science and law; these journals, such as APA's *Law and Human Behavior*, mix law and psychology, and they operate more like standard psychology journals.

Speeches to Legal Audiences

All of the expert witness advice applies here, except concerning the adversarial tone. Although no educated audience suffers fools gladly, we have found legal audiences to be receptive and no more hostile than most other academic settings. Speaking to legal audiences compels you to avoid or at least minimize jargon and to provide accessible examples to illustrate the more technical points you wish to make. Speaking to legal audiences in a nonadversarial context can be an especially effective way of educating a captive and inquisitive audience of lawyers and judges.

Applicable Research

Getting involved in litigation has generated some of our favorite research ideas to take back to the lab. The problems that people litigate give new perspective on what our field knows and where the gaps are. For Fiske, one such revelation was that most stereotyping research concerned peers judging peers, but the most consequential prejudice is inflicted by the more powerful on the less powerful (e.g., hiring and promotion decisions; Fiske, 1993). For Borgida, gaps in the research literature revealed by legal questions during a trial stimulated experiments on the behavioral consequences of priming men to view women as sexual objects (Rudman & Borgida, 1995). The research was cited in *Jenson v. Eveleth Taconite Co.* (1993), the first federal class action sexual harassment case in the United States (see Bingham & Gansler, 2002). The insight we gain through getting involved in litigation can lead not only to intriguing new research directions but also to research questions that are directly relevant to the arguments litigators seek to make, which enhances our ability to translate those findings back to the legal realm (providing research evidence that litigators can readily use to make those very points).

Contract Research

Doing contract research is a different ballgame than basic but applicable research. Attorneys may hire researchers to conduct studies directly relevant to trying a particular case. For example, attorneys may request surveys of the public that generates the jury pool, questions to ask potential jurors during jury selection (voir dire), and even studies within an organization involved in the lawsuit. One caveat: Although as a well-trained social scientist, you have the skills and knowledge to conduct these kinds of research studies, you can't usually publish contract research, so you have to decide the best use of your time and expertise. Contract research typically will be very specific to more particular, applied questions that define aspects of the legal case (e.g., how do people perceive the actual trademark brand in dispute?), as opposed to being a theory-driven investigation.

Beyond these defined roles, psychological scientists are being asked to consult and advise legal professionals all the time. In light of all the opportunities that might come your way, we encourage you to follow your interests and to pursue what interests you. But we recommend that you first ask trusted colleagues (e.g., faculty mentor, department chair) whether this kind of professional engagement will count as service or outreach—or not at all, perhaps even against you as a serious academic. Their answers will help you to make an informed decision about involvement, which is especially important if this work won't count for tenure, promotion, or raises. Some have argued that "public service should be a central component of what it means to be a scientist" (Rosenberg et al., 2015, p. 966), but not all departments share this belief. Also, don't sell your valuable time cheaply; think about what the lawyers are being paid and what kind of compensation would appropriately acknowledge your time and effort (see Brodsky & Gutheil, 2016, for a wide-ranging set of expert witness guidelines).

CONCLUSION

Nowadays researchers work in a climate of skepticism about the brain and behavioral sciences, whereby politics and advocacy can distort scientific evidence (Kaslow, 2015). Communicating effectively and clearly in this climate, especially to nonacademic audiences, has become crucial to the survival of our scientific species. Whether in a policy or legal context, we endorse Eagly's (2016) view that social scientists should serve as honest brokers. The central message of our chapter is that the process—*how* honest brokers do their educating—is crucial. You need to write what you know, write what the field knows, and anticipate the ways in which your work will be critiqued. You must take extra steps to document all your sources and to be direct, clear, and firm in your communications. Above all else, remember to communicate in such a way that you preserve the integrity of the science you proffer. In the legal arena, as in the policy arena, "Offering bad science or misrepresenting scientific findings can come back to bite scientists when political [or legal] opponents figure out how defective the science–policy [science–law] relation is" (Eagly, 2016, p. 22).

REFERENCES

Bingham, C., & Gansler, L. L. (2002). *Class action: The landmark case that changed sexual harassment law*. New York, NY: Anchor Books.

Blount, R. (2015a, February 13). Minnesota Duluth women's hockey coach Shannon Miller says dismissal violates Title IX. *Star Tribune*. Retrieved from http://www.startribune.com/umd-coach-shannon-miller-dismissal-violates-title-ix/291785391/#1

Blount, R. (2015b, September 28). 3 former Duluth coaches file discrimination lawsuit. *Star Tribune*. Retrieved from http://www.startribune.com/3-former-duluth-coaches-file-discrimination-lawsuit/329788221

Borgida, E., & Fiske, S. T. (Eds.). (2008). *Psychological science in the courtroom: Beyond common sense*. London, England: Blackwell.

Brodsky, S. L., & Gutheil, T. G. (2016). *The expert expert witness: More maxims and guidelines for testifying in court* (2nd ed.). http://dx.doi.org/10.1037/14732-000

Brown v. Board of Education of Topeka, 347 U.S. 483 (1954).

Ceci, S. J., & Bruck, M. (2006). Children's suggestibility: Characteristics and mechanisms. *Advances in child development and behavior, 34*, 247–281. http://dx.doi.org/10.1016/S0065-2407(06)80009-1

Daubert v. Merrell Dow Pharmaceuticals, 509 U.S. 579, 113 S.Ct. 2786, 125 L.Ed. 2d 469, (U.S. Jun 28, 1993) (No. 92-102).

Eagly, A. H. (2016). When passionate advocates meet research on diversity, does the honest broker stand a chance? *Journal of Social Issues, 72*, 199–222. http://dx.doi.org/10.1111/josi.12163

Fiske, S. T. (1993). Controlling other people. The impact of power on stereotyping. *American Psychologist, 48*, 621–628. http://dx.doi.org/10.1037/0003-066X.48.6.621

Fiske, S. T., & Borgida, E. (2011a). Best practices: How to evaluate psychological science for use by organizations. *Research in Organizational Behavior, 31*, 253–275. http://dx.doi.org/10.1016/j.riob.2011.10.003

Fiske, S. T., & Borgida, E. (2011b). Standards for using social psychological evidence in employment discrimination cases. *Temple Law Review, 83*, 867–876.

Fiske, S. T., & Dupree, C. H. (2014). Gaining trust as well as respect in communicating to motivated audiences about science topics. *PNAS: Proceedings of the*

National Academy of Sciences of the United States of America, 111 (Suppl. 4), 13593–13597.

General Electric Co. v. Joiner, 522 U.S. 136 (1997).

Grice, P. (1975). Logic and conversation. In D. Davidson & G. Harman (Eds.), *The logic of grammar* (pp. 64–75). Encino, CA: Dickenson.

Hopkins v. Price Waterhouse, 618 F. Supp. 1109 (D. D.C. 1985).

Jenson v. Eveleth Taconite Co., 824 F. Supp. 847 (D. Minn. 1993).

Kaslow, N. J. (2015). Translating psychological science to the public. *American Psychologist, 70*, 361–371. http://dx.doi.org/10.1037/a0039448

Kassin, S. M. (2015). The social psychology of false confessions. *Social Issues and Policy Review, 9*, 25–51. http://dx.doi.org/10.1111/sipr.12009

Kumho Tire Co., Ltd. v. Carmichael, 526 U.S. 137, 119 S.Ct. 1167, 143 L.Ed. 2d 238 (U.S. Mar 23, 1999) (No. 97-1709).

Rosenberg, A. A., Branscomb, L. M., Eady, V., Frumhoff, P. C., Goldman, G. T., Halpern, M., . . . Wexler, C. (2015). Congress's attacks on science-based rules. *Science, 348*, 964–966. http://dx.doi.org/10.1126/science.aab2939

Rudman, L. A., & Borgida, E. (1995). The afterglow of construct accessibility: The behavioral consequences of priming men to view women as sexual objects. *Journal of Experimental Social Psychology, 31*, 493–517. http://dx.doi.org/10.1006/jesp.1995.1022

United States Code. (2015). *Title 28, Appendix—Rules of Evidence.* Washington DC: U.S. Government Printing Office.

Wells, G. L. (2016). Eyewitness identification. In D. Faigman, D. Kaye, M. Saks, & J. Sanders (Eds.), *Modern scientific evidence: The law and science of expert testimony* (pp. 451–479). St. Paul, MN: West.

7

Law Enforcement:
Finding Common Purpose

Jack Glaser and Amanda Charbonneau

During a ride-along with a police officer in a major U.S. city, one of us (JG) found himself being conveyed rapidly toward the scene of a reported crime in progress. Listening to the police radio, the police officers and I could hear that multiple units were responding. As we arrived at the scene, the dispatcher noted that a plainclothes officer would be in the vicinity, and she described what he was wearing and his vehicle. It became all the more clear that approaching the scene of a crime in progress can be dangerous for police officers. One of the dangers is that they, especially if out of uniform, will be mistaken for suspects; their efforts to help could be misconstrued by other responding officers as threatening, sometimes with lethal consequences. Police officers have been the mistaken targets of force by other officers, and in the wake of two prominent cases of fatal shootings of off-duty officers by on-duty officers in New York, the state's governor appointed a task force to study this phenomenon. The task force

http://dx.doi.org/10.1037/0000066-008
Making Research Matter: A Psychologist's Guide to Public Engagement, L. R. Tropp (Editor)

identified 10 cases in the United States between 1981 and 2009 wherein off-duty officers were fatally shot by on-duty officers (New York State Task Force on Police-on-Police Shootings, 2010). Although roughly three quarters of patrol officers in the United States are White (Reaves, 2015), only one of those fatally shot was White. Eight were African American and one was Latino.

This troubling pattern of racial disparities is, of course, consistent with broader patterns of use of force on civilians (Fryer, 2016; Goff, Lloyd, Geller, Raphael, & Glaser, 2016; Nix, Campbell, Byers, & Alpert, 2017) as well as dramatic racial disparities in the much more common (thousands per day) cases of pedestrian and vehicle stops and searches (Glaser, 2015; Jones-Brown, Gill, & Trone, 2010). The racial disparities in law enforcement contact necessarily cause and exacerbate disparities in criminal justice sanctions (Glaser, 2006) and no doubt undermine trust for (and, therefore, cooperation with) law enforcement in communities of color (Tyler & Huo, 2002). Racial disparities in policing can be in part explained by social psychological research on implicit stereotypes linking Black people with crime and weapons (e.g., Eberhardt, Goff, Purdie, & Davies, 2004; Payne, 2001) and showing how racial stereotypes affect shooting behavior (Correll, Park, Judd, & Wittenbrink, 2002; Glaser & Knowles, 2008) even among police officers (Correll et al., 2007; Plant & Peruche, 2005).

In contrast to the gross racial disparities in fatalities for off-duty officers, the New York State task force found that the racial disparities in treatment by police were far less pronounced in cases where out-of-uniform officers were on duty (i.e., undercover or plainclothes). One of the possible explanations the task force offered was that departments have policies and procedures for indicating that on-duty officers who are out of uniform are in the vicinity and what those officers look like. This was demonstrated vividly on the previously mentioned ride-along. Sure enough, at the scene of the crime (an active situation with officers in pursuit of suspects) the plainclothes officer and his car clearly matched the description provided by the dispatcher and he and the other officers on the scene were able to signal each other.

This episode reflects a larger theme of this chapter, that engagement by psychological scientists with law enforcement is mutually beneficial.

Police benefit from the application of established psychological principles to a set of challenges that are inherently cognitive, affective, motivational, behavioral, and social in nature. Psychological science benefits from studying psychological principles in a domain that is highly important but also where effects of judgments and decisions are concrete, palpable, and, increasingly, measured. In this chapter, we explore this theme in depth and, bearing the multiple and mutual benefits in mind, discuss how scientists can connect and collaborate with law enforcement agencies and officials and how to have an effect on policing and on the populations that are policed.

WHAT BENEFITS CAN BE GAINED FROM WORKING WITH LAW ENFORCEMENT?

Conducting research in, about, or for an applied domain can be mutually beneficial to the researchers (and their fields) and relevant practitioners, but certain characteristics of policing make it particularly so. Policing is saturated with psychological phenomena, including goals and motives, attitudes, behavior, emotions, perception, attention, memory, judgment and decision making, interpersonal relations, power, aggression, intergroup processes, and organizational behavior. Researchers benefit from investigating these phenomena in relation to police judgments and behaviors that are well-documented and have immediate, tangible effects (e.g., stop, search, use of force, arrest). Therefore, the effects of these behaviors (and, indirectly, of the policies, practices, processes, and interventions relating to them) are readily (although by no means perfectly) traceable. For example, racial stereotyping effects in policing result in discernible disparities in stop, search, arrest, and use-of-force rates (Glaser, 2015).

A note about the documentation of policing data: What analysts and other interested parties refer to as crime data are often actually arrest data. Actual rates of offending for most types of crimes are unknown, except for the estimates that can be imputed from the random sampling used in the National Crime Victimization Survey. For those law enforcement agencies that regularly collect and report data on contacts with civilians that fall short of arrest (e.g., stops, searches, warnings, citations, use of force), the data are only as reliable as the extent to which officers comply in reporting the information, and the data's utility can also be limited by the design of the data collection instruments, policies, and procedures. That said, significant strides are being made in the breadth and quality of policing data collection and analysis; for example, California's recent passage of AB953, the Racial and Identity Profiling Act of 2015, could represent a substantial advance in policy requiring police data reporting from every department in the largest U.S. state.

Such developments in documentation and data collection will help social scientists make stronger inferences about the causal effects of psychological variables on law enforcement outcomes. As an example, the Center for Policing Equity's (CPE's) National Justice Database[1] is recruiting scores of police departments to share data on pedestrian and vehicle stops, searches, and use of force, which will be combined with data on departmental culture and climate, policy landscape, census, crime, measures of officers' attitudes, and other data to provide multimethod and multilevel analyses. To be clear, the goal here is not to have access to these data simply to benefit psychologists or other social scientists; rather, what ultimately matters is how these data can be used to benefit civilians, officers, and police departments.

Benefits to Civilians

Civilians and the general public can benefit greatly from the application of established principles in psychology to understanding and changing police behaviors that are highly consequential for their lives. Short-sighted policies and biased decisions by police can cause some communities to be underprotected and overpoliced (i.e., stopped and searched at unjustifiably high rates). Overpolicing has collateral effects, including lower levels of trust in police and other authorities, and therefore reduced

---

[1] The first author is a principal investigator on the National Justice Database (NJD) project and a member of the board of directors of the Center for Policing Equity. The second author is a participating researcher on the NJD.

cooperation (e.g., during investigations). Members of racial minority communities who get arrested and convicted at disproportionate rates as a result of racial profiling also experience collateral effects in employment, income, and health, and they are typically disenfranchised from voting, which has far-reaching implications for the representation of their communities in our political system. The broader public also stands to benefit from psychologically informed policing through enhanced public safety, reduced costs associated with mass incarceration, and reduced social unrest that results from racial tensions and distrust.

Benefits to Officers

The benefits and relevance of psychological research to police officers' professional and personal lives are also substantial. Patrol officers in particular are almost constantly required to make decisions and take action under conditions of considerable uncertainty, which are known to promote heuristic processing and undermine rationality (Tversky & Kahneman, 1974). The pervasive ambiguity and uncertainty in the police officer decision-making environment is reflected in the very low rates at which possession of contraband or weapons is revealed in searches that are predicated on suspicion of those very crimes (Goel, Rao, & Shroff, 2015; Jones-Brown et al., 2010). Anecdotally, officers report a psychological toll from having to spend so much of their working time looking for bad behavior, a habit that some indicate follows them into their personal lives, disrupting their relationships. Use of lethal force is traumatizing for officers and can be a career-ending event, thereby leading to considerable professional and psychological costs. Accordingly, psychological research and expertise offer opportunities for improving officer safety, job satisfaction, and quality of life.

Benefits to Police Departments

Police departments and related government agencies can benefit not only from the application of psychological theory and research to their work but also from psychologists' expertise in defining and operationalizing concepts. As psychology researchers, we take great pains to define and measure relevant psychological concepts (e.g., attitudes, beliefs, motivations, emotions) accurately and to operationalize them meaningfully in our surveys and experiments. We apply standards for causal inference that include rigorous assessments of the validity of the concepts we study, the statistical procedures we use, the conclusions we draw, and the ways in which we extrapolate findings to people and settings outside those of a particular study.

In formal policies and daily practices, many concepts in police work are poorly defined, to the detriment of police departments' ability to act consistently and effectively and to supervise and maintain accountability. For example, most police departments (as well as most states) have formal prohibitions on racial profiling, but definitions of profiling vary widely, with many defining *profiling* as using race or ethnicity as the sole basis of suspicion—a premise that renders the definition useless in practice. Similarly, reasonable suspicion is the essential legal standard determining when someone may be detained and/or searched by the police, yet this concept is very vaguely defined in both case law and departments' policies and trainings. The domains of racial profiling and reasonable suspicion are two examples among many where law enforcement policies, procedures, and practices could benefit greatly from the more precise understanding of those concepts derived from psychological science.

In fact, psychological scientists can and do help the law enforcement field define and operationalize these concepts to promote fairer and better policing. For example, we and other social scientists have advised police departments and helped to develop legislation (e.g., Racial and Identity Profiling Act of 2015) based on more precise, actionable definitions of racial profiling. Furthermore, we are currently conducting research to better understand the nature of suspicion as a psychological construct and reasonable suspicion as a practicable legal construct (Charbonneau & Glaser, 2016). As we bring psychological research, theory, and clarity of definitions of concepts to policing, we also bring considerable expertise in a range of survey, experimental, modeling, and statistical methods that can promote better understanding of police performance and effectively test for best practices.

HOW TO CONNECT AND COLLABORATE WITH LAW ENFORCEMENT

In undertaking collaborations with law enforcement entities, researchers must appreciate the diverse perspectives of the individuals, agencies, unions, and institutions with whom they work, while leveraging their own training and expertise. Psychological and other social sciences have developed and tested theories that explain a great deal about human behavior and decision making, yet practitioners rarely have access or exposure to these theories. As such, it would serve us well to keep a few principles in mind as we seek opportunities to connect and collaborate with law enforcement.

Find Common Purpose

When law enforcement leaders become aware of the potential benefits of applying psychological research and principles to their work, they tend to be receptive to collaborating with researchers. Their motives, like anyone's, are likely to be mixed. They are genuinely motivated to deliver effective and fair policing to the communities they serve, but political pressure, bad publicity, and the threat of litigation also encourage police departments to turn to academics. In some cases, departments turn to researchers after a tragic event like the shooting of an unarmed individual, whereas in other cases court-appointed independent monitors have instructed departments to collaborate with researchers to investigate inequities in policing practices. Given their varied interests and training, researchers and law enforcement leaders will need to identify common goals at the outset of any collaborative effort. These goals might include improving policing, increasing public and officer safety, and promoting fairness. Law enforcement leaders may value fairness in principle because it improves policing and public safety or simply because it reduces the number of complaints and threat of litigation. Either way, understanding these goals will help researchers in establishing a foundation for the collaboration.

Learn Policing Practices and Culture

In addition to identifying common goals with police departments, researchers will need to orient themselves to policing practices and departmental culture. Collaborations between social scientists and law enforcement practitioners require consistent bidirectional education and sharing of expertise. Without such insight, psychologists and other social scientists run the risk of pursuing research questions that are largely irrelevant or unlikely to generate actionable knowledge.

Researchers can participate in a number of activities to ground their work in the practical and political realities of law enforcement, including site visits and interviews, ride-alongs, attending community academies[2] and departmental trainings and meetings, reviewing policies and procedures, and attending relevant city council and community meetings. In addition to orienting researchers to the policy landscape, culture, and day-to-day practices in a particular law enforcement entity, these activities will direct their attention to domains in which psychological theory and research methods are particularly relevant. For example, conversations with and observations of police while on duty readily reveal that officers are often in the position of providing services more appropriately carried out by a social worker or mental health professional. As another example, observation of officers on the job quickly reveals the high degree of discretion they have in deciding where and when to patrol, which lends itself

---

[2] Community academies provide a version of the training new cadets receive that is geared toward helping civilians gain insight into policing practices.

to relying on heuristics (see Chaiken, Liberman, & Eagly, 1989) as they engage with civilians.

Be Strategic and Realistic

Efforts to understand the relevance of psychological science and methods and finding ways to collaborate with law enforcement will be all the more effective if interested researchers understand and respond strategically and realistically to the organizational cultures and policies they encounter. For example, some problems in law enforcement (as in any other domain) are largely logistical or technological; a department that is understaffed or poorly equipped may well benefit from psychological insights but may not have adequate personpower to address them or may have more pressing root problems with which to contend.

Like other industries, policing is also very much influenced by tradition and leadership. To further complicate matters, there is considerable turnover in police leadership: Police chiefs serve at the discretion of mayors and city managers and, consequently, their stability can be at the mercy of local politics. Departures can be precipitous, derailing plans for research and reform. Organizational conditions are not always amenable to change, so acting when policy windows are open is highly advantageous; recent public focus on policing has opened windows for changes in policies and practices and for the inclusion of psychological expertise.

Although law enforcement agencies have a finite set of formally documented policies, guidelines, training standards, accountability structures, and intraorganizational relationships, they also have robust informal influences, including departmental culture, informational channels, and undocumented practices and norms. Often, the line between the formal and informal processes will be blurry. For example, department policy and trainings may include very specific definitions of reasonable suspicion, but daily briefings emphasizing expectations for numbers of civilian stops and arrests might compel officers to stretch or narrow those definitions.

Play to Your Strengths

Researchers should also play to their strengths as they seek to build collaborations with law enforcement and maximize the potential of bridging the gap between theory and practice. Although serving as a general psychological or methodological expert may be tempting, to the extent that an agency or group of agencies faces a problem for which a researcher's particular expertise is relevant, a researcher should focus energy on that. It should come as no surprise, then, that much of the social psychological research on policing has addressed racial stereotyping, prejudice, and discrimination (e.g., Correll et al., 2002; Eberhardt et al., 2004; Glaser & Knowles, 2008; Plant & Peruche, 2005). This is an area of strength for the field dating back nearly a century, and racial bias is a problem that has vexed policing and society for centuries. Much of our own engagement with police has centered on issues associated with racial bias (e.g., Glaser, 2015; Spencer, Charbonneau, & Glaser, 2016), allowing us to leverage our expertise in theory, methodology, and research findings in ways that have value for officers and departments seeking to address racial bias in policing.

As another example, many departments undertake community-oriented policing activities, such as sending officers to community events or to meet with residents in informal settings. A researcher familiar with contact theory would quickly identify these practices as an opportunity to increase positive contact between police officers and residents, which has the potential to reduce bias-based policing (see Broadus, 2015; Pettigrew & Tropp, 2011). For example, the researcher might suggest increasing the number of officers who participate in these activities as well as adjusting the types of community activities in which they engage; in turn, police chiefs and community leaders could then identify opportunities and barriers to implementing such changes. Another well-developed area of theory and research that has been applied to policing is procedural justice and legitimacy (e.g., Braga, Winship, Tyler, Fagan, & Meares, 2014; Tyler, Fagan, & Geller, 2014; Tyler & Huo, 2002). Drawing on the insight that being treated fairly is at least as important to people as the outcomes they receive, this work has been used with considerable effect by police and other law enforcement agencies who seek to build trust with and cooperation from the communities they serve.

Adopt a Policy-Analytic Approach

Generally speaking, when bringing research to bear on a policy domain, it is tremendously helpful to apply a systematic, policy-analytic approach such as Bardach's popular Eightfold Path (see Bardach & Patashnik, 2015). This approach starts with defining the problem carefully and precisely and avoiding defining the problem around a desired (or readily available) solution. Policy analysis requires the consultant and the client to confront the trade-offs—no policy or change in practice will completely solve a problem, and some will cost more than others (in terms of dollars, political capital, human capital, etc.). In policy analysis and design it is crucial to be mindful of actionableness, feasibility, and windows of opportunity. Recommendations can make sense in terms of psychological theory, but the parties with whom you are working may not be in a position to take action or influence those who are. As with any conscientious advising, it is important to establish a relationship with your law enforcement partners that is cooperative and trust based but has as a fundamental principle an understanding that you will tell the agency what it needs to hear, which may or may not be what it wants to hear. It is best to communicate this early on in the partnership, so that all parties have a shared understanding of respective roles and responsibilities.

Clarify How Research Can Be Described and Used

It is also important to make clear to law enforcement leaders what research involves and the different ways in which it can be described and used. Regrettably, some contractors offering psychology-based trainings for police (e.g., to address implicit bias) describe their work as "evidence based," yet this ambiguous term is wide open for interpretation. Quite reasonably, many people will interpret the term to mean that the trainings have been tested and shown to deliver the promised or strongly implied results. Often, however, the term is used to mean that the trainings were developed on the basis of a body of research evidence supporting the underlying psychological principles that are being presented. In applying psychological theory to law enforcement, researchers should differentiate between research evidence supporting a particular psychological principle that is used as the basis for developing a training or intervention and research evidence that directly indicates the effectiveness of a specific training or intervention. Research evidence supporting a particular psychological principle will likely include laboratory studies and might include studies from a range of applied fields and may or may not demonstrate direct links to behavior. Though still vitally important, this evidence base should not be conflated with one that demonstrates that a particular type of intervention (e.g., training, change in policy) has led to a desired effect.

Although this distinction will seem obvious to many researchers because of their training, many practitioners will not be accustomed to the distinction. Consider the preceding example regarding community policing and the research literature on intergroup contact. A police chief might be interested in demonstrating to stakeholders that increasing the number of officers involved in community-based activities will decrease the number of civilian complaints against officers. Although the researcher can point to a compelling body of research evidence indicating that positive contact between members of different groups reduces biased behavior, there may be no rigorous evaluation demonstrating a precise causal effect of increasing the number of officers who participate in community activities on civilian complaints. This illustrative example represents an increasingly common scenario: Criminal justice agencies and private funders are actively pursuing rigorous evaluations and randomized controlled trials toward the development of evidence-based practices. These institutions therefore turn to academic researchers because of our expertise in study design, data collection, statistical analyses, and causal inference. We must, however, continue to explain how (a) developing policies and interventions based on research-supported principles (e.g., intergroup contact reduces bias, implicit biases cause discriminatory behaviors) is superior to basing those on instinct or intuition alone and (b) evaluating the effectiveness of those policies and interventions can be worthwhile points of connection and collaboration between academic researchers and law enforcement.

HOW CAN COLLABORATIONS WITH LAW ENFORCEMENT BE STRUCTURED MOST EFFECTIVELY?

In light of the range of issues faced by law enforcement agencies, a team of interdisciplinary researchers with varied methodological training may be best equipped to address some of the more vexing questions about policing. The CPE creates an infrastructure that allows academic researchers from a range of fields and police departments to collaborate on a multitude of projects. The National Justice Database, CPE's largest endeavor, is collecting standardized data on officers' contact with civilians and use of force from many police departments throughout North America. This particular collaboration brings social psychologists, economists, demographers, and policy researchers together to work on complex questions about racial disparities in civilian contact and use of force using a variety of experimental and observational research methods. Together, interdisciplinary teams of researchers analyze data on officers' contact with civilians and data gathered through psychological measures (e.g., questionnaires and indirect measures of implicit biases), community demographic variables, departmental climate assessments, and analyses of policies, procedures, and trainings. CPE has accrued considerable expertise in working with police department leadership and unions, and it centralizes administrative processes, thereby easing the burden of establishing collaborations for both the researchers and police departments. At the same time, collaborations between researchers and law enforcement agencies can take other forms. Some researchers work directly with individual departments on projects that vary greatly in size and scope, and there can be advantages to these focused collaborations, particularly if they can help to solve local problems (with their structural and political idiosyncrasies), if not scale to other locales.

Although some researchers will embrace working with police departments, others may have concerns regarding this kind of collaborative research (e.g., loss of objectivity) and may be more comfortable studying policing from a distance. They face trade-offs in this decision, however. They will find it much harder to understand law enforcement processes and make their research matter. It is possible, however, to study law enforcement by working directly with police without becoming coopted by their interests. In fact, there are varied and even conflicting interests within agencies. Command staff, rank-and-file officers, unions, and internal affairs departments may have very different perspectives on any number of policing practices. Although it is possible to conduct research that is relevant to, even useful for, policing without engaging directly with law enforcement agencies, much is to be gained in collaboration.

Moreover, police departments are not the only type of institution that seeks counsel from psychological experts regarding law enforcement practices. The courts, independent monitors, mayors' offices, civilian oversight commissions and review boards, legislatures, state and federal departments of justice, and other advocates all seek input from researchers and play an important role in the policies and practices that are adopted by departments. While their perspectives and specific goals will vary, all of these stakeholders share an interest in research that has direct implications for law enforcement policies and practices.

CONCLUSION

The effects of policing are often immediate and sometimes dire, and they represent the front line of civilians' contact with governing authority and the entry point to the criminal justice system. Policing done well (e.g., with an emphasis on fairness and positive community contact) can enhance public safety and a sense of community, but policing done poorly can have detrimental effects that reverberate through society and often rebound to the responsible agencies. Psychologists interested in conducting research on and in collaboration with law enforcement officials and agencies are well positioned to spark relationships of considerable mutual benefit. Researchers gain opportunities to better understand human psychology in an important and fascinating domain where the consequences of judgment and behavior are very concrete. Law enforcement partners stand to gain a wealth of hard-won scientific knowledge about individual, group, intergroup, and organizational processes that can help them to address vexing problems and improve their performance. Currently, much law enforcement is based on lay theories of human psychology, so those developing policies, procedures, and practices stand to benefit from a more systematic, empirically supported understanding of human behavior. On the other hand, law enforcement officials are, in very important ways, operating in environments that are profoundly different from those in which psychologists typically work and in which prior psychological research has been conducted. As such, psychological scientists working with law enforcement will do well to seek direct experience and to conduct research with police through mutual exchanges of information and feedback in sustained collaboration.

REFERENCES

Bardach, E., & Patashnik, E. M. (2015). *A practical guide for policy analysis: The eightfold path to more effective problem solving.* Thousand Oaks, CA: CQ Press.

Braga, A. A., Winship, C., Tyler, T. R., Fagan, J., & Meares, T. L. (2014). The salience of social contextual factors in appraisals of police interactions with citizens: A randomized factorial experiment. *Journal of Quantitative Criminology, 30,* 599–627. http://dx.doi.org/10.1007/s10940-014-9216-7

Broadus, J. (2015, Fall). Can contact theory offer lessons for police-community relationships? A review of the literature, best practices, and challenges. *Policy Matters Journal, 13*(2), pp. 43–47.

Chaiken, S., Liberman, A., & Eagly, A. H. (1989). Heuristic and systematic information processing within and beyond the persuasion context. In J. Uleman & J. Bargh (Eds.), *Unintended thought* (pp. 212–252). New York, NY: Guilford Press.

Charbonneau, A., & Glaser, J. (2016, January). *Defining and measuring criminal suspicion.* Datablitz talk at the Psychology and Law Preconference for the Society for Personality and Social Psychology, San Diego, CA.

Correll, J., Park, B., Judd, C. M., & Wittenbrink, B. (2002). The police officer's dilemma: Using ethnicity to disambiguate potentially threatening individuals. *Journal of Personality and Social Psychology, 83,* 1314–1329. http://dx.doi.org/10.1037/0022-3514.83.6.1314

Correll, J., Park, B., Judd, C. M., Wittenbrink, B., Sadler, M. S., & Keesee, T. (2007). Across the thin blue line: Police officers and racial bias in the decision to shoot. *Journal of Personality and Social Psychology, 92,* 1006–1023. http://dx.doi.org/10.1037/0022-3514.92.6.1006

Eberhardt, J. L., Goff, P. A., Purdie, V. J., & Davies, P. G. (2004). Seeing Black: Race, crime, and visual processing. *Journal of Personality and Social Psychology, 87,* 876–893. http://dx.doi.org/10.1037/0022-3514.87.6.876

Fryer, R. G., Jr. (2016). *An empirical analysis of racial differences in police use of force* (NBER Working Paper No. 22399). Cambridge, MA: National Bureau of Economic Research. http://dx.doi.org/10.3386/w22399

Glaser, J. (2006). The efficacy and effect of racial profiling: A mathematical simulation approach. *Journal of Policy Analysis and Management, 25,* 395–416. http://dx.doi.org/10.1002/pam.20178

Glaser, J. (2015). *Suspect race: Causes and consequences of racial profiling.* New York, NY: Oxford University Press.

Glaser, J., & Knowles, E. D. (2008). Implicit motivation to control prejudice. *Journal of Experimental Social Psychology, 44,* 164–172. http://dx.doi.org/10.1016/j.jesp.2007.01.002

Goel, S., Rao, J. M., & Shroff, R. (2015). *Precinct or prejudice? Understanding racial disparities in New York City's stop-and-frisk policy* (SSRN Scholarly Paper No. ID 2572718). Rochester, NY: Social Science Research Network. Retrieved from http://papers.ssrn.com/abstract=2572718

Goff, P. A., Lloyd, T., Geller, A., Raphael, S., & Glaser, J. (2016). *The science of justice: Race, arrests, and police use of force.* Los Angeles, CA: Center for Policing Equity. Retrieved from http://policingequity.org/wp-content/uploads/2016/07/CPE_SoJ_Race-Arrests-UoF_2016-07-08-1130.pdf

Jones-Brown, D. D., Gill, J., & Trone, J. (2010). *Stop, question and frisk policing practices in New York City: A primer.* New York, NY: Center on Race, Crime and Justice, John Jay College of Criminal Justice. Retrieved from https://static.prisonpolicy.org/scans/PRIMER_electronic_version.pdf

New York State Task Force on Police-on-Police Shootings. (2010). *Reducing inherent danger: Report of the Task Force on Police-on-police Shootings.* Retrieved from https://www.hks.harvard.edu/criminaljustice-backup/publications/Police-on-Police_Shootings.pdf

Nix, J., Campbell, B. A., Byers, E. H., & Alpert, G. P. (2017). A bird's eye view of civilians killed by police in 2015: Further evidence of implicit bias. *Criminology & Public Policy, 16,* 309–340.

Payne, B. K. (2001). Prejudice and perception: The role of automatic and controlled processes in misperceiving a weapon. *Journal of Personality and Social Psychology, 81,* 1–12.

Pettigrew, T. F., & Tropp, L. R. (2011). *When groups meet: The dynamics of intergroup contact.* New York, NY: Psychology Press.

Plant, E. A., & Peruche, B. M. (2005). The consequences of race for police officers' responses to criminal suspects. *Psychological Science, 16,* 180–183. http://dx.doi.org/10.1111/j.0956-7976.2005.00800.x

Racial and Identity Profiling Act of 2015, Pub. L. No. AB953, § Chapter 466 12525.5 (Government Code), 13012 and 13519.4 (Penal Code), California Government and Penal Codes (2015).

Reaves, B. A. (2015). *Local police departments, 2013: Personnel, policies, and practices* (Law Enforcement Management and Administrative Statistics). Washington, DC: Bureau of Justice Statistics. Retrieved from https://www.bjs.gov/index.cfm?ty=pbdetail&iid=5279

Spencer, K. B., Charbonneau, A. K., & Glaser, J. (2016). Implicit bias and policing. *Social and Personality Psychology Compass, 10,* 50–63. http://dx.doi.org/10.1111/spc3.12210

Tversky, A., & Kahneman, D. (1974). Judgment under uncertainty: Heuristics and biases. *Science, 185,* 1124–1131. http://dx.doi.org/10.1126/science.185.4157.1124

Tyler, T. R., Fagan, J., & Geller, A. (2014). Street stops and police legitimacy: Teachable moments in young urban men's legal socialization. *Journal of Empirical Legal Studies, 11,* 751–785. https://doi.org/10.1111/jels.12055

Tyler, T. R., & Huo, Y. J. (2002). *Trust in the law: Encouraging public cooperation with the police and courts.* New York, NY: Russell Sage Foundation.

8

Education: Building Trusted Partnerships With Schools

Geoffrey Maruyama and Lara Westerhof

A recent poll showed that a majority of Americans are dissatisfied with the quality of education in the United States (Gallup, 2015); this same poll found that 80% of responding parents have children attending public schools, and three fourths of the parents are satisfied with the schools their children attend. The conflicting numbers illustrate the complexity of the challenges faced by schools, educators, and researchers working across the educational system. These challenges provoke disparate, important, challenging, and researchable questions, for example, Are our schools successful, or not? How do we measure success? How do media shape the ways people view schools? If our schools aren't successful, what responsibility do educators have for lack of success? And if our

The contents of this chapter were developed in part under Grant #P116140033 from the Fund for the Improvement of Postsecondary Education, First in the World program, the U.S. Department of Education. However, the contents do not necessarily represent the policy of the U.S. Department of Education, and endorsement by the federal government should not be assumed. We appreciate comments from Dr. Suzanne Russ, Dr. Andrew Furco, and Dr. Linda R. Tropp.

http://dx.doi.org/10.1037/0000066-009
Making Research Matter: A Psychologist's Guide to Public Engagement, L. R. Tropp (Editor)

schools are inferior, why do so many people from other countries send their children to study here?

Education has always been important, but it is even more so in our information age. An educated workforce with skills that include knowledge, creativity, innovativeness, effective decision making, and efficiency is essential to our nation's economic as well as societal success. People broadly agree that the quality of our lives in the future depends on the success of our education system. Nonetheless, U.S. education is too often described in terms like "education crisis" or "failing American schools" (e.g., Chuck, 2013; Klein, 2011; Lynch, 2015).

Moreover, schools today face their most diverse student populations ever, with increasing numbers of students coming from groups that have tended to do less well in our education system. Schools are being asked to take on multiple roles to provide students with an array of critical supports (nutrition, health, social adjustment, even shelter) needed to be successful. As such, our responsibilities for educating the children of this country represent the intersection of self-interest, national needs, and social good, guided by principles that include fairness, equal opportunity, social justice, and, in some cases, the American Dream.

Within this societal landscape, many psychologists and other social and behavioral science researchers work with schools. For them, we draw on our experiences to describe principles of collaboration when working with schools, articulate some of the challenges that can emerge, discuss action research as a framework that can guide engagement, and provide examples from our work to illustrate how effective school partnerships can develop.

WHAT PRINCIPLES CAN GUIDE ME IN DEVELOPING EFFECTIVE PARTNERSHIPS WITH SCHOOLS?

Because every partnership reflects the partners and contexts involved, each researcher needs to determine how best to apply the principles outlined here to their own work.

Complex Dynamics and Inconsistent Findings Are Challenging and Take Time to Address

Schools are not simple places. Their many adult components (e.g., leadership, teachers, professional community, curriculum) affect students, and their students' experiences and backgrounds (e.g., language, race/ethnicity, class, gender) affect adults, producing findings that can vary widely across settings and circumstances. Despite the complexities, a number of generalizable effects have been reported (e.g., cooperative learning; Johnson & Johnson, 2009). Their infrequency, however, shows that developing insightful research studies and effective interventions takes time. The educational problems our schools face are likely to defy simple or quick solutions, so researchers need to be willing to commit to long-term partnerships and sustained effort.

Schools Don't Need Saviors, but Partners

If you think you can be a savior, you need more experience in schools before you do research with them. Researchers who go into schools thinking that they have all the answers are likely to be met with skepticism and distrust, for the professionals in school settings have been thinking about the issues for much longer and in more complex and nuanced ways than have most researchers. They know their setting and its quirks and dynamics. It makes sense for researchers to develop partnerships, sharing ownership and responsibility rather than assuming a role as the expert. Indeed, many types of complementary expertise are needed to design and execute effective school-based research.

Commitment of all partners to the work is key to producing the kinds of outcomes that are possible. Without mutual commitment, interventions will be compromised and/or poorly implemented, not necessarily through malice, but due to other commitments and demands within school settings. For example, statewide testing might occur during a time that was expected to be used for implementing a key part of an intervention and preempt the intervention.

Trust Is Essential

Also integral to establishing an effective partnership is building *trust* in the relationship. In the context of a school–university partnership, *trust* refers to the belief that each member will commit to the partnership, bring expertise, and help other members meet their goals (Kruger, Davies, Eckersley, Newell, & Cherednichenko, 2009). Although distrust is common in the beginning of a partnership, trust can be fostered over time and with effort through the development of mutual respect and valuing one another's expertise and contributions (Kruger et al., 2009; McLaughlin & Black-Hawkins, 2004) and by shared goals identified or developed across partners (Hord, 1986; Schlechty & Whitford, 1988; Sirotnik, 1988). Trust is also promoted by effective communication (MacDonald & Dorr, 2006; McLaughlin & Black-Hawkins, 2004), which requires sustainable interactions across all partners (e.g., university faculty and administrators, school administrators and educators) and positive, supportive interactions among partners. When conflicts arise later, as is likely, trust is deepened when all partners accept shared ownership of problems and resolve issues in a timely manner through critical but respectful discussions (Kirschner, Dickinson, & Blosser, 1996). If problems are not resolved, the success and longevity of the partnership can suffer.

Engage All Partners From the Start—and Throughout Your Work Together

True collaboration involves engaging partners from the very beginning—including in formulating the particular issue to be studied and developing the approach (e.g., Lewin, 1948). Engagement throughout and after the research process shows respect for partners and helps develop and sustain commitment to the partnership. Partnership goals must be specific enough to implement the research as intended yet general enough to allow for flexibility and change (Clark, 1988); identifying goals that are either too specific or too general could strain the partnership and may even result in its dissolution (Sirotnik & Goodlad, 1988).

Before you embark on a partnership, find out about your partners' needs and goals, and find an intersection between your needs and goals and theirs. Sharing goals and perspectives and identifying needs are central to school-based research partnerships, for they shape and guide the research process from beginning to end. The research plan and design should meet various partners' needs and goals as well as identify each partner's roles and responsibilities consistent with their strengths and expertise. Inclusive planning lays the foundation for all partners' involvement, defining how different partners will be involved in different stages of the research process. For example, educator partners may be actively involved in collecting surveys from students or training school staff to conduct interviews or facilitate focus groups. Partners can also provide important insights in interpreting data, such as by offering more information about the school context or by identifying themes from qualitative data.

You will also want to plan how and when research findings are shared with your partners (and other stakeholders) to maximize the practical utility of the research for them and the communities they serve. Your partners may also have a unique advantage in disseminating findings to the community (see Chapter 10, this volume), for they are often well connected to parents and other community members, who likely trust local educators more than they trust an unfamiliar university researcher. This can increase community buy-in for your work, strengthen your partnership, and create the potential for future projects.

Understand the Setting and Culture

Researchers also need to develop an understanding of the students and schools with which they will be working and to appreciate the specific nature of the challenges they face before finalizing research plans. Researchers need to attend to the varying cultures in the educational setting within which they will be working, including the history of the school, the relationship between the school and surrounding neighborhoods—and whether the school is a crossroads between different neighborhoods with competing values, the culture(s) of students, the kind of professional community the teachers and staff have created, and the structure of leadership within the school building and among authority leaders. Unlike more traditional, lab-based settings in which researchers work, in field-based settings researchers often have limited control over their conditions or what happens within them (e.g., Schon, 1995).

In addition to developing a richer understanding of local conditions, psychologists need to reflect on how university cultures differ from school cultures. University cultures typically value reflection, analysis, and scientific inquiry as well as creation of theory and generalizable knowledge. In contrast, school cultures necessarily value practical knowledge with applicability to the classroom setting, focusing on identifying effective practices that make a difference in the local setting (Schlechty & Whitford, 1988; Thorkildsen & Scott Stein, 1996). People from schools may initially view university goals and values as incompatible with their own goals and values. School staff may perceive university researchers as being too theoretical and more concerned with publications and recognition than with discovering solutions to the challenges staff face in educating students. School staff may also feel that their practical knowledge is not respected as valid or important. Researchers may feel teachers are dismissive of their academic scholarship and theoretical expertise. Such views can hamper exchanges between university and school partners (Kirschner et al., 1996), and both school and university staff must learn to respect each partner's unique expertise and hard work (Clark, 1988).

WHAT CHALLENGES MIGHT I ENCOUNTER IN WORKING WITH SCHOOLS?

In the beginning of a new partnership, your school partner will likely have a range of questions and concerns about your burgeoning relationship. Most teachers view their everyday responsibilities as being of greater importance than any research partnership (e.g., Kruger et al., 2009), so participation in a research partnership may be viewed as a distraction from primary responsibilities and possibly disruptive to routines the school has established (Clark, 1988). School staff also may be wary of the time commitments associated with research and potential assumptions researchers might make about class time. For example, presuming that teachers can easily accommodate survey distribution in their classes may be seen as disrespectful of the culture and nature of pre-K–12 education, because teachers face pressure to cover a great deal in the limited time they have with students. Setting aside time for research involves more than just completing a survey; additional time is needed to prepare students, explain and administer the survey, and follow up if there are questions. Teachers may also be concerned about their ability to explain the research if parents or others have questions. If you worry that your school partner has such a concern, ask what you can do to support teachers and minimize any burdens introduced by the research.

Educators also likely will have questions stemming from prior experiences with university researchers. Ask them whether they have worked with university researchers before—and if they have, ask them how it went and what could be done to help things go smoothly. Understanding their prior history with school–university partnerships is important for forging an effective, trusting relationship and better comprehending their perspectives.

WHAT APPROACH CAN GUIDE ME IN DEVELOPING SCHOOL–RESEARCH PARTNERSHIPS?

Now that we have suggested some basic principles to lay the groundwork for developing effective partnerships and have mentioned common challenges, we next briefly describe *action research* as a methodological approach for working collaboratively with schools (Lewin, 1948). We then describe ways of lessening burden for school partners, discuss different types of partnerships that one might develop, illustrate the principles and models we have outlined by describing some work that we have done, and finally, note changes in higher education that would better support school–university partnerships in conducting engaged research.

The field of psychology has approaches that are well established and well suited for developing sustainable partnerships with educators and schools. Most notably, action research (Lewin, 1948) provides researchers with tools and approaches for creating effective partnerships between experts in theory and experts in practice. Lewin (1948) argued that each type of expertise needed to be acknowledged, for each was integral to successful partnerships. What makes Lewin's work compelling for partnership work is his view of action research as a vehicle for creating social advancement and change.

In addition to his emphasis on unique areas of expertise, Lewin's (1948) conceptualization of action research highlighted the cyclical and long-term nature of processes involved in partnership work. Lewin believed that researchers and practitioners should together review results, reflect on the findings and processes of research, and reformulate ideas for future work, ultimately using the completed work to inform future projects. Researchers interested in working with schools and educators need to recognize that practical problems are unlikely to be solved in any single study, which makes school-based research cyclical in nature. For example, if a research project identifies an ineffective component of a school-based intervention, the school partner will likely want to explore this weakness in future studies, rather than ending the partnership or examining another area of study altogether.

WHAT CAN WE DO TO FACILITATE SUCCESSFUL PARTNERSHIPS WITH SCHOOLS?

To facilitate successful partnerships with schools, you should first learn whether the research question is important or of value to the school you are asking to partner with you. If your work isn't important for their goals, then no matter how much they like you or how valuable your work may be, they are not a good match for you. Find out what they care about and the outcomes for which they will be held accountable. If what you want to do aligns with and helps them accomplish their goals, it will be relatively easy for them to work with you.

Second, once you have identified appropriate school partners, then you should determine the potential benefits of collaboration for all partners. Helping partners reach their goals is good, but other benefits might be of equal importance, such as providing support for staff, offering workshops that meet certification requirements, providing teachers with access to instructional materials, or helping them evaluate the effectiveness of particular programs. Other possible benefits might include using your research skills to help them analyze data in new and different ways to evaluate their programs or to help them defuse interpersonal conflicts among students in the classroom.

Third, focus on minimizing the amount of classroom disruption that the research time will create. Class time is precious and has many demands on it. Don't expect to have much free class time turned over to you for your research. To the extent possible, see if you can conduct your research while either you or the teacher is providing instruction that covers material that needs to be covered.

Fourth, provide support for educators working with you. This could mean providing release time for teachers to plan the research and review the findings or providing a person to help with class during the research. In some instances, help by providing a trained member of the research team (especially one who is a certified teacher) to conduct the research or manage the classroom, thereby making the experience less taxing for teachers.

Finally, there is what we hope is common courtesy. Recognize that school partners are busy professionals whose time is as important as is yours. Unless they offer to do these tasks, show your respect for teachers and school staff by not asking them to copy materials, to be responsible for collecting measurement instruments, or to be the ones to answer students' questions. Compensation of some type for teachers' extra time and effort is also appreciated (e.g., we have provided gift cards for interview participation).

WHAT KIND OF PARTNERSHIP WITH SCHOOLS SHOULD I SEEK?

When developing a school–university research partnership, you must decide what type of relationship you want to cultivate. You may seek a *cooperative relationship* in which two or more institutions agree to work together but in which university researchers typically lead the research while school partners observe or play a supportive role in facilitating the work. One specific type of cooperative relationship is consultation, wherein researchers are clearly recognized as experts who share knowledge with school practitioners (McLaughlin & Black-Hawkins, 2004; Ravid & Handler, 2001).

Alternatively, you may seek a *collaborative relationship* in which partners equitably share responsibility, authority, and ownership (see Clark, 1988; Hord, 1986). This type of partnership requires more investment by researchers than does a cooperative relationship but tends to be more sustainable (Kruger et al., 2009). Here, researchers work with school practitioners as equal partners in setting partner roles and expectations, and school practitioners exercise greater responsibilities for certain aspects of the research, such that all members actively contribute to the research process (Ravid & Handler, 2001). Because collaborations require close, trusting relationships, they can help partners effectively navigate obstacles and extend the partnership beyond a single study (McLaughlin & Black-Hawkins, 2004; Ravid & Handler, 2001).

Another type of collaborative relationship is an umbrella partnership. It includes multiple collaborative partnerships organized within a larger umbrella organization. Researchers and educators are represented, as are other stakeholders, such as community members and families. The umbrella approach is much larger and more complex than other partnership models and requires greater resources and institutional support (it can be used for university-level relationships), often including memoranda of understanding (or agreement) that define the circumstances and nature of the partnership as well as resource commitments of the partners to facilitate the development of subordinate relationships. When successful, umbrella partnerships tend to produce long-term efforts and effects with greater impact (McLaughlin & Black-Hawkins, 2004; Ravid & Handler, 2001) and facilitate studies under the umbrella.

Partnership types can be categorized further by their particular characteristics. Important dimensions include how they are structured (e.g., who leads, who else is involved), their purposes (e.g., to improve available programs for youth), and the roles of and expectations for different partners. These dimensions can help provide perspectives for researchers to develop customized partnerships, with each partnership developing its own unique and effective practices over time (MacDonald & Dorr, 2006).

Adopting any specific partnership model is rarely enough to guarantee everyone's engagement in the research process for school–university partnerships. Success of partnerships is largely dependent on the extent to which partners are engaged, are committed to the work, and make time to participate. Cooperative models implicitly tell practitioners that they are not equal contributors, so, if you need greater engagement, such models are likely to be lacking. However, even in collaborative models one might find it challenging to manage partners' involvement; open, critical discussions are often necessary to establish more equal relationships (Fine & Torre, 2004). In some instances, designating leaders from each institution who agree with and are invested in the larger mission of the partnership will help encourage positive, supportive interactions across institutions and increase buy-in for the partnership (Clark, 1988). In addition, partnerships benefit from "early wins"—tangible products that can create pride and satisfaction (e.g., research findings or reports)—for they may keep partners motivated and engaged (Sirotnik & Goodlad, 1988).

A RESEARCH EXAMPLE ILLUSTRATING HOW TO WORK WITH SCHOOLS

To illustrate how partnerships with schools can work, we describe collaborative projects we have done in the area of educational equity and fairness. As part of broader work on educational disparities (e.g., Maruyama, 2003), Maruyama (2012) became interested in metrics—such as the ACT college readiness assessment—for determining whether or not students are ready for college. Because he was part of a state-level education partnership in Minnesota, he had access to college performance data as well as ACT scores; these data showed that the ACT was a poor predictor of college performance (Maruyama, 2012), bringing claims that the ACT test predicts college readiness into question.

These findings led to an ongoing search for better predictors of college success, with a focus on measures from high school course performance (e.g., Chan & Maruyama, 2014). We developed collaborative partnerships with school districts interested in college (and career) readiness. We worked in partnership with school curriculum staff as well as staff from district research, evaluation, and assessment offices. This issue is central to their goals, for schools are required to measure and report on college readiness, and imprecise outcomes that make them look bad can be damaging. In particular, our focus has been on whether or not course grades could provide better predictors than metrics such as the ACT, for grades in principle are based on observing behavior over a long period using multiple approaches. Because states are adopting sets of standards for courses that define the content that teachers need to cover in specific courses, there are opportunities to increase consistency and predictive value of grades. We have therefore begun to see how well standards-based grades (SBGs) predict future performance and college readiness.

We found partners for this work both because we already had built collaborative partnerships with school districts and because they shared our interests in finding metrics to measure development of college readiness for their diverse student populations. We drew on a long-standing partnership with a large, urban school district in Minnesota to look at SBGs. The work is mixed-methods, examining SBG practices among high school mathematics teachers. Our collaborative relationships with practitioners across the district helped us identify the right research questions, connect with potential participants, and interpret our results. Teacher interviews helped identify important components of the setting.

We began this project with a minimally invasive archival analysis examining the relation between already existing standards-based grading and student achievement. This gave us background knowledge while minimizing burden for schools and teachers. Rather than working independently on the analyses and simply sharing findings with the district, we initially held collaborative, working meetings with the high school mathematics coordinator and staff within the district's research, evaluation, and assessment (REA) office to develop an engaged approach. School personnel were able to provide context for our data that ultimately proved key to interpreting our findings and the ability to identify the teachers who were implementing SBGs, as well as how long they had been using

SBGs. The high school mathematics coordinator categorized individual teachers across the district by level of experience with standards-based grading and described different grading practices and expectations across high schools. The REA staff also shared districtwide trends that allowed us to put our findings into context; they removed identifying information so we had deidentified archival data that made it easier to gain approval processes from the relevant review boards. Without having built a partnership and a collaborative approach, we doubt that they would have been willing to share the information.

As noted above, we conducted semistructured interviews with high school mathematics teachers to examine why they had (or had not) used standards-based grading and, if so, how they were using standards-based grading. Initially, we drafted questions guided by existing research literature and shared them with the high school mathematics coordinator during a working meeting. We spent the meeting reworking our interview questions, removing those that were superfluous or would likely seem naive, confusing, or unimportant to teachers, and adding others suited for and unique to the context of the schools and district. Sharing perspectives increased the value of the interviews for our partners and made the interviews more relevant due to their greater understanding of the district and how it operates.

Our collaborative relationships also proved valuable for recruiting teacher participants and gathering data. The high school mathematics coordinator, who worked closely with high school mathematics teachers across the district, went out of her way to support our research by introducing this project to teachers and encouraging them to participate in our study. Not only did this personal contact bolster our response rate, it also helped us build rapport and trust with teachers during the interviews, which ultimately helped us to collect valid and richer data. Teachers reported that SBGs were just as easy to give as traditional grades. Further, teachers using SBGs did not want to go back to traditional grading systems. Prediction analyses found SBGs somewhat better than traditional grades in predicting later high school grades, but the findings were mixed. Both sets of findings led us to ongoing work focused on providing professional development for teachers to help them use SBGs in more consistent ways.

CONCLUDING THOUGHTS

Universities and researchers need to recognize the fundamental importance of partnerships with pre-K–12 schools and their dependence on them, for universities ideally only accept high school graduates who are ready for college and for preparation for the workforce and careers. Further, the mission of urban-focused and land grant institutions in a 21st-century urban age demands participation in addressing educational challenges. For many other institutions of higher education, such partnerships represent a commitment to being good and responsible citizens in our communities and to creating public good. Universities provide for many schools and communities the single greatest resource available to help address local challenges and lessen inequalities that damage the social fabric and quality of life for everyone (see Wilkinson & Pickett, 2009).

Our experiences have led us to believe that if we really want to make meaningful progress in addressing key educational issues, we must pay close attention to how school–university research partnerships are structured and the roles that universities can play in facilitating successful partnerships. Those of us willing to engage in partnerships with schools must remind our institutions why these kinds of endeavors are of value and warrant collective support. Challenges, including complexity, lack of control, and a dynamic and changing environment, should be recognized (e.g., Schon, 1995), and faculty should be encouraged and supported rather than be left to feel at risk of being denied tenure or being viewed as less productive.

Universities are generally not structured to create and support collaborative, long-term research addressing important and complex practical problems, for their structure largely rewards individual accomplishment and theoretical advance and allows researchers latitude in deciding what they want to study. Lack of focused attention to practical and important societal issues diminishes the institutional capacity of universities to produce impactful and meaningful work that can benefit schools, communities, and the broader society (Leiderman, Furco, Zapf, & Goss, 2003; Marullo & Edwards, 2000). But we believe and hope that is changing. As public scrutiny and accountability increase, universities need translational engaged research that can help highlight the value of partnerships with schools.

We believe that changing university norms and culture not only will enhance the ability of researchers to engage with constituencies such as schools but also could have salutary effects on higher education, creating in college graduates and graduate students a greater commitment to personal actions and research that enrich the public good and build within the academy an understanding of the importance of translational research and collectively addressing inequalities in society. By dealing directly and visibly with issues such as the impact of poverty and social inequality in schools, universities can help build stronger pathways to college success for underserved populations while reaffirming the centrality of institutions of higher education in creating a better future for all. For higher education institutions, mutually beneficial school–university partnerships have great potential to create engaged, public-minded citizens that society needs for democracy to flourish and to compete globally in the 21st century.

REFERENCES

Chan, C.-K., & Maruyama, G. (2014, April). *The relations of high school math preparation, college remediation and college completion.* Paper presented at the Annual Meeting of the American Educational Research Association, Philadelphia, PA.

Chuck, E. (2013, October 8). US in a "real state of crisis," education secretary says. *NBC News.* Retrieved from http://www.nbcnews.com/news/other/us-real-state-crisis-education-secretary-says-f8C11354527

Clark, R. W. (1988). School-university relationships: An interpretive review. In K. A. Sirotnik & J. I. Goodlad (Eds.), *School-university partnerships in action: Concepts, cases, and concerns* (pp. 32–65). New York, NY: Teachers College Press.

Fine, M., & Torre, M. E. (2004). Re-membering exclusions: Participatory action research in public institutions. *Qualitative Research in Psychology, 1,* 15–37.

Gallup. (2015). Education. Retrieved from http://www.gallup.com/poll/1612/Education.aspx

Hord, S. M. (1986). A synthesis of research on organizational collaboration. *Educational Leadership, 43*(5), 22–26.

Johnson, D. W., & Johnson, R. T. (2009). An educational psychology success story: Social interdependence theory and cooperative learning. *Educational Researcher, 38*, 365–379. http://dx.doi.org/10.3102/0013189X09339057

Kirschner, B. W., Dickinson, R., & Blosser, C. (1996). From cooperation to collaboration: The changing culture of a school/university partnership. *Theory Into Practice, 35*, 205–213. http://dx.doi.org/10.1080/00405849609543724

Klein, J. (2011, June). The failure of American schools. *The Atlantic*. Retrieved from http://www.theatlantic.com/magazine/archive/2011/06/the-failure-of-american-schools/308497

Kruger, T., Davies, A., Eckersley, B., Newell, F., & Cherednichenko, B. (2009, March). *Effective and sustainable university-school partnerships: Beyond determined efforts by inspired individuals.* Canberra, Australia: Teaching Australia.

Leiderman, S., Furco, A., Zapf, J., & Goss, M. (2003). *Building partnerships with college campuses: Community perspectives.* Washington, DC: Council of Independent Colleges.

Lewin, K. (1948). Action research and minority problems. In G. W. Lewin, *Resolving social problems* (pp. 201–216). New York, NY: Harper & Row.

Lynch, M. (2015, August 27). 10 reasons the U.S. education system is failing [Blog post]. Retrieved from http://blogs.edweek.org/edweek/education_futures/2015/08/10_reasons_the_us_education_system_is_failing.html

MacDonald, M. F., & Dorr, A. (2006). *Inside school-university partnerships: Successful collaborations to improve high school student achievement.* Los Angeles: Los Angeles County Office of Education and University of California.

Marullo, S., & Edwards, B. (2000). From charity to social justice: The potential of university-community collaboration for social change. *American Behavioral Scientist, 43*, 895–912. http://dx.doi.org/10.1177/00027640021955540

Maruyama, G. (2003). Disparities in educational opportunities and outcomes: What do we know and what can we do? *Journal of Social Issues, 59*, 653–676. http://dx.doi.org/10.1111/1540-4560.00083

Maruyama, G. (2012). Assessing college readiness: Should we be satisfied with ACT or other threshold scores? *Educational Researcher, 41*, 252–261. http://dx.doi.org/10.3102/0013189X12455095

McLaughlin, C., & Black-Hawkins, K. (2004). A schools-university research partnership: Understandings, models and complexities. *Journal of In-Service Education, 30*, 265–284.

Ravid, R., & Handler, M. G. (Eds.). (2001). *The many faces of school-university collaboration: Characteristics of successful partnerships.* Englewood, CO: Teacher Ideas Press.

Schlechty, P. C., & Whitford, L. (1988). Shared problems and shared vision: Organic collaboration. In K. A. Sirotnik & J. I. Goodlad (Eds.), *School-university partnerships in action: Concepts, cases, and concerns* (pp. 191–204). New York, NY: Teachers College Press.

Schon, D. A. (1995). Knowing in action: The new scholarship requires a new epistemology. *Change, 27*(6), 26–34.

Sirotnik, K. A. (1988). The meaning and conduct of inquiry in school-university partnerships. In K. A. Sirotnik & J. I. Goodlad (Eds.), *School-university partnerships in action: Concepts, cases, and concerns* (pp. 169–190). New York, NY: Teachers College Press.

Sirotnik, K. A., & Goodlad, J. I. (Eds.). (1988). *School-university partnerships in action: Concepts, cases, and concerns.* New York, NY: Teachers College Press.

Thorkildsen, R., & Scott Stein, M. R. (1996). Fundamental characteristics of successful university-school partnerships. *The School Community Journal, 6*(2), 79–92.

Wilkinson, R., & Pickett, K. (2009). *The spirit level: Why more equal societies almost always do better.* London, England: Bloomsbury.

9

Health Professionals: Conducting Research With Physicians

Louis A. Penner

The goal of this chapter is to share some lessons learned about research collaborations between psychologists and physicians. Hopefully, the information provided will make such collaborations easier and more productive for research psychologists who want to conduct research in medical settings and collaborate with physicians in this activity. However, my contribution to this book begins with a full disclosure. I suspect that many of the other contributors either prepared for a career doing applied, translational research or found it was a logical progression of the path their career was taking. In contrast, the setting in which I now find myself is, in many ways, not a logical progression of my career path. Rather like a lot of good things that have happened to me over the past 46 years, finding myself as a

Preparation of this chapter was partially supported by the following awards: National Cancer Institute (NCI) 1U54CA153606-01, T. Albrecht and R. Chapman, co–principal investigators; NCI P30CA022453 Cancer Center Support Grant, G. Bepler, principal investigator; NCI 1RO1CA138981, L. Penner, principal investigator.

http://dx.doi.org/10.1037/0000066-010
Making Research Matter: A Psychologist's Guide to Public Engagement, L. R. Tropp (Editor)

social psychology researcher in a large cancer center is the product of some very good luck for which I can claim very little credit.

A bit of background is needed. About halfway through the third decade of my career, two things happened. First, the state of Florida practically begged me to retire by dangling a very large lump sum payout in front of me if I would only stop doing what I had been doing (teaching and research in a psychology department). Despite grave misgivings, I accepted this carrot, uncertain what I would do after this early retirement. But shortly thereafter dame fortune smiled on me yet again when my wife, Teri Albrecht, was offered the job she had always wanted, indeed dreamed of—starting a brand new program in communication and behavioral oncology at the Karmanos Cancer Institute (KCI) located at Wayne State University, in Detroit, Michigan. I was offered and accepted a position as a professor of oncology as well as senior scientist within this program. KCI is a National Cancer Institute–Designated Comprehensive Cancer Center, one of 45 such centers in the United States. Importantly for this chapter, the cancer center had no history of behavioral research. When we arrived, we soon discovered that although the center director had a strong interest in behavioral research, the physicians and basic science faculty pretty much had no interest in anything that involved behavioral approaches to either cancer treatment or prevention.

Perhaps the biggest and most pleasant surprise since I made an abrupt turn in my career is that the skills and knowledge I had acquired as a traditional social psychologist, especially those in design and data analysis, were invaluable in this new, very different setting. The terms used in this new research area are often quite different from those I used, and the specific foci of the research are often entirely new, but the skills and knowledge I brought with me could easily be applied to the new research context in which I found myself and permitted me to arrive at valid answers to some very distinct research questions. I now have an even more positive perspective on the value of the training research psychologists receive during graduate school; we have something very important to contribute.

Of course, there is widespread interest in the medical community in certain social problems that are health related. One of these is health disparities between people from different racial or ethnic groups. However, this problem is typically not approached from a social psychological perspective. Indeed, when most physicians talk about health disparities, they are actually talking about health-related biological or genetic differences between populations that are typically not preventable, such as differences between population groups in the incidence and/or prevalence of some disease or how the disease presents itself once a person has been diagnosed. In contrast, as a social psychologist I am interested in how social factors affect interactions between physician and patients and the impact of these interactions on both physicians' and patients' health care decisions (e.g., recommending a certain treatment, adhering to that treatment). The underlying model that guides most of my work, greatly simplified, is that physician and patient social attitudes (specifically race-related attitudes) affect how they perceive medical interactions and how physicians and patients communicate during these interactions. These, in turn, can affect outcomes of these interactions, such as physician and patient treatment decisions and patient adherence to these decisions.

The central question addressed in this chapter is, then: How does a mainstream traditional social psychology researcher become a successful researcher in a medical setting? Indeed, how does someone primarily trained to do laboratory experiments and analyze questionnaires meaningfully contribute to both applied and basic health-related research in collaboration with physicians? As I explore this topic, we must recognize the vast difference between physicians who work in primary care or other less specialized practices in community settings and the physicians in an academic medical setting, with whom I work. Effectively working with different categories of physicians requires different strategies and I can only talk about my own experiences. So, I hope the issues I write about in this chapter are to some degree generalizable to interactions with other health care providers in other contexts, though the setting in which I work has many unique aspects. Thus, as would be the case with findings from basic laboratory research, one must empirically determine the generalizability of one's experiences and insights across settings.

WHAT MOTIVATES AN ACADEMIC LIKE ME TO WORK WITH PHYSICIANS?

Even before I moved to KCI, I had decided that collaborating with my wife in her work on physician–patient communication during their conversations about cancer treatments (e.g., Albrecht et al., 2003) might be a way for me to move back to studying the kinds of phenomena that motivated me to become a social psychologist in the first place. I became a social psychologist primarily as a way to meld my strong feelings about certain social issues with a career in research. Specifically, I wanted to understand the origins of racial and ethnic prejudice and discrimination and perhaps provide some solutions to these social problems. Many years later, the specific social problem that has interested me is the substantial disparities in the quality of health care White and Black cancer patients receive (Penner et al., 2012). When I started this line of research I was, of course, aware that economic and social factors at a societal level result in certain groups of people receiving poorer health care, but I believed that beyond that were subtle but powerful phenomena that caused physicians to provide better care to some patients than others and, at the same time, caused some patients to make better decisions about their health care than did others. So, I was, in some ways, primed for the move before it occurred.

At about the same time I moved to Detroit and KCI, the Institute of Medicine (IOM) published its landmark volume *Unequal Treatment* (Smedley, Stith, & Nelson, 2003). The IOM charged a panel of distinguished medical and behavioral researchers with the task of determining why the health of members of most racial and ethnic minority groups was so much poorer than that of the White majority. Up until perhaps 40 years or 50 years earlier, the answer would have focused on biological differences between races (Byrd & Clayton, 2001). Indeed, until about the 1930s, a widely endorsed medical theory was that Blacks and Whites were two different species and the former was biologically inferior to the latter.[1] Such blatantly racist theories had passed into history by the time of the

---

[1] This was one of the "scientific" reasons for the infamous Tuskegee syphilis study (Jones, 1993).

IOM panel. However, most people expected the IOM panel to identify the causes of health disparities as factors such as differences in the availability of insurance, levels of health literacy, lifestyle (e.g., diet, exercise), and specific health-related behaviors (e.g., routine health screenings). And, indeed, some of these factors receive significant notice in their report. The panel, however, surprised most people when it proposed that the major reason why racial and ethnic minorities as a group are less healthy than majorities is because they receive poorer health care. Even more startling to many, the panel concluded that one of the major causes of these health care disparities was the social attitudes of both health care providers and their patients. Specifically, racial stereotypes, prejudice, discrimination among health care providers, as well as mistrust among patients, result in many members of racial or ethnic minorities receiving poorer health care than do majority group members. There was one problem, however: They had little if any data to support this argument.

I had spent much of my career studying these kinds of variables in one form or another. And as I mentioned earlier, personally and professionally I was committed to addressing these kinds of social problems. So, I was highly motivated to address racial health care disparities, and by virtue of my training and experiences as a research social psychologist, I had the tools necessary to meaningfully study the role of race-related attitudes, beliefs, and behaviors in these inequities. Further, I had been placed in an almost perfect "laboratory" to study them.

WHAT MOTIVATES PHYSICIANS TO COLLABORATE WITH A RESEARCHER LIKE ME?

Some physicians share my interest in racial and ethnic disparities in health care; however, most physicians where I work are medical oncologists who take a primarily biological or medical approach to a person's health status. Although they certainly recognize the importance of lifestyle (e.g., exercise, diet, stress) to a person's health, the notion that social factors and the quality of communication between them and their patients might affect health outcomes is not typically on their radar.

Furthermore, most physicians believe they are free of any racial bias that would influence how they interact with a patient—and even if they were biased in some way, they would be inclined to believe that they could control it. At an explicit, conscious level they usually can, but bias also operates at an implicit or automatic level. In the past 5 to 10 years, my research colleagues and I (Hagiwara et al., 2013; Penner, Blair, Albrecht, & Dovidio, 2014) have rather persuasively demonstrated that implicit racial bias can affect how non-Black physicians communicate with their Black patients and how these patients feel about them and the interaction. More recently, we have found that physicians' implicit racial bias can affect how optimistic or pessimistic Black patients are about a recommended cancer treatment (Penner, Dovidio, et al., 2016). Although many of my physician colleagues are aware of and interested in this work, it is often hard for many of them to think beyond their own individual interactions with patients and appreciate the broader cumulative effects of factors that may subtly affect how they or their patients feel and how such factors may ultimately affect their patients' health.

So, what motivates them to work with a researcher like me (or my colleagues)? For most of the oncologists with whom we work, the first step toward a collaboration with them is their becoming aware of a very practical problem in the delivery of care to their patients. This awareness is most likely to occur among physicians with administrative positions who are inclined to look at the problem in the aggregate.[2] For example, my colleague Susan Eggly is about to start a large behavioral intervention with the goal of increasing minority patient enrollment in prostate cancer clinical trials. She has the enthusiastic support of several collaborators at two hospitals, including physicians with administrative roles, in large part because these individuals were already quite aware of and concerned about the relative dearth of Blacks enrolled in such trials. When physicians become aware of such problems, they are then quite open to behavioral interventions to address them and are willing to work with research collaborators. Similarly, my wife and I were able to establish very productive research collaborations

---

[2] Presentations (grand rounds) are another way to do this. The presentations must clearly identify the medical relevance of what you plan to study. However, because members of my group often study problems in health care, we must be very careful not to criticize or indict those who deliver this health care.

with two successive division chiefs of a pediatric hematology/oncology clinic (see Harper et al., 2014; Penner, Guevarra, et al., 2016; Peterson et al., 2014) because we focused on a problem that already concerned them: psychological distress among both parents and their children due to the invasive and stressful cancer treatments children must receive.

HOW CAN I BUILD SUCCESSFUL COLLABORATIONS WITH PHYSICIANS?

As I have already noted, most oncologists have little if any background in social and behavioral research. Some are initially bemused by this kind of research and others are outright skeptical of it. It's a fool's errand to approach them from the perspective of a social psychologist interested in subtle causes of a social problem of which they may not even be aware. So what does one do? The primary answers to this question involve doing certain things even before you approach a physician about a specific project.

As is true in any research collaboration, first your collaborators must know you either personally or professionally—that is, they must be aware of you and your work. However, the odds that a physician would read psychology journals are beyond minuscule, and thus they must get to know you or at least know someone who knows you. If you are not involved in clinical practice, it may be difficult to get to know the physicians on staff because the avenues for establishing personal relationships with them are quite limited. On the days they have clinic hours, they are simply too busy for informal meetings such as a lunch or coffee. Outside of medical schools, faculty meetings may provide opportunities for dialogues, but in medical schools such meetings are infrequent and are incredibly hierarchical events, in which you are part of an audience rather than a group of interacting colleagues. Thus, there are few opportunities to informally get to know your new medical colleagues.

Identify the Skills You Have to Offer

So, other avenues to establish relationships with physicians must be found. One may be to offer help in areas where you have expertise that they may need. In my case, I found a point of connection through my expertise in psychometrics and measurement. Today, tests of almost any new drug must be accompanied by patient-reported outcomes, which concern how the disease and/or its treatment affects the patient's quality of life. More specifically, quality-of-life questions are mostly about adverse effects of the treatment (e.g., fatigue, nausea) and the physical symptoms of the disease. Academic physicians are well trained in understanding physical measurements, such as the levels of toxins in a cancer patient's blood or the images of tumors that are produced by computed tomography scans. They have little if any training, however, in the measurement of variables that are indicators of constructs or latent factors. As a result, they typically lack the expertise needed to obtain reliable and valid self-report data. Thus, when I first arrived, I made myself available to my physician colleagues as a psychometrician and helped to design quality-of-life questionnaires. My contributions in these areas opened up personal conversations with physicians that made subsequent collaborations more likely.

Obtain Funding to Support the Collaboration

Knowing a physician at a personal level is a necessary but not sufficient condition for a research collaboration. In academic medical centers, especially a National Cancer Institute–designated comprehensive cancer center, there is really only one way to develop an actual research collaboration with a physician: applying for or receiving federal grants for research projects. Grants are the coin of the realm, and you have little credibility or opportunity for collaborations if you are not grant funded. So, the first thing a psychologist working in an academic medical setting must do is pursue and obtain grants. There is a very simple reason why grants are needed for collaborations with physicians: In almost all academic medical settings, faculty must generate some substantial portion of their salary from either clinical fees or grant support. Further, there are typically no resources for research unless they can be paid for with money from grants. Thus, the possibility of a research collaboration is essentially zero unless one obtains a grant to support the collaborative work.

In addition, receiving grants helps you to get noticed, and grants give you credibility when you approach other physicians about collaborative projects. Furthermore, suggesting a grant collaboration to a physician provides leverage that you might need to engage them in your projects. Specifically, if you are invited to be a coinvestigator on a large National Institutes of Health grant, physicians will be motivated to listen to what your research is about and to at least consider becoming a part of it.

State Goals in Terms of What Physicians Value

However, like anyone else, physicians will not be really motivated to collaborate on a project unless they think it is of value. Thus, although virtually all research collaborations in an academic medical setting are centered on grants, it is not enough to simply offer physicians and other health care professionals a role in these grants. They must see value in the effort.

A key factor that motivates physicians and other health care providers to collaborate is the perception that, if the grant is successful, it will improve clinical practice, especially the specific kind of clinical practice in which they are engaged. In most instances, physicians will not be motivated to collaborate by the kinds of theoretical questions often asked by social psychologists (e.g., How can we minimize the effects of racial bias?). Rather, they will be motivated by a practical problem (e.g., How can we advance the delivery of high-quality medical care to racially and ethnically diverse populations?). It is incumbent on us as social psychology researchers to frame the questions in terms of what physicians care more about, thereby convincing them that the issues we wish to study will help them to address the practical problems they want to solve.

In summary, it is fairly unlikely (though not impossible) that a physician or other health professional will be the one to initiate a research collaboration with a research psychologist. In most instances you must approach them for the purpose of establishing such a collaboration. They must either know you directly or know the person who suggested the meeting; they must see you as a serious researcher (i.e., know that you have received grants); and most important, you must propose something that is seen as of fairly direct value to the delivery of clinical services or to the clinical research mission (e.g., clinical trials) of the facility at which they work. In academic medical centers, most clinicians are also researchers (doing what is often very basic research), but when a research psychologist approaches them, the problem of interest must be a quite practical one, and the closer it is to their own clinical interests, the more likely a collaboration.

WHAT CHALLENGES MIGHT I ENCOUNTER IN WORKING WITH PHYSICIANS?

If one wants to study racial disparities in health care in a real-world medical setting, one must, of course, collaborate at some level with physicians and other health professionals. However, in candor, I must say that when I began to develop a research program on health care disparities, I worked primarily with other social psychologists (e.g., Penner et al., 2014) and my colleagues in the Communication and Behavioral Oncology Program at KCI, who also have backgrounds in psychology and communication theory and research. The reason for this is fairly simple: Just as most social psychologists do not having the training or expertise to study, say, the genetic basis of lung cancer, most physicians do not have the training or expertise to study, say, the impact of perceived racism on a patient's response to treatment recommendations (Penner et al., 2009). Indeed, as mentioned earlier, most physicians receive little or no training on how to study such problems (Hamel et al., 2015; Hardeman et al., 2015). Thus, many physicians will likely be uncomfortable with a study in which the primary variable of interest is a latent variable such as implicit racial bias or perceived social support.

Many physicians may be familiar with psychologists who provide adjunct clinical services (e.g., neurological testing, psychotherapy) to the patients they treat. However, few of them have ever had a professional, collaborative relationship with a research psychologist. Their specific concerns about projects proposed by research psychologists will likely vary as a function of the particular setting and research question. However, the concern that I confront most commonly is that carrying out behavioral studies, which usually have no immediate direct therapeutic benefits for their patients, will somehow interfere with the delivery of needed clinical services. Over 90% of the research I do is hospital based, which means I need to collect data in clinics that provide treatment to people with serious health problems. Because other revenue sources (e.g., federal grants) have declined, physicians in most hospital-based clinics are under considerable pressure to treat large numbers of patients in the most cost-efficient ways possible. The people responsible for these clinics do not want long waiting times for their patients and really do not want anything to delay or disrupt physician interactions with patients. As a result, physicians and other health professionals are wary of anything that might disrupt their schedule of appointments with patients, or what they refer to as the "clinic flow." For example, during one of the first times I was in a clinic collecting data, I was startled by a physician who came out of a consultation room and screamed at me that I was delaying his seeing a patient because the patient was completing one of our questionnaires; he was mistaken and later apologized, but it was a stark introduction to doing behavioral research in an active clinic. In the pediatric hematology/oncology clinic where my research colleagues and I studied families' psychological reactions to pediatric cancer, our research assistants were publicly chastised (and humiliated) on multiple occasions by a physician who was convinced that somehow they were interfering with patient treatment in the clinic. The division chief apologized profusely, but he could do nothing to prevent the next occurrence. In most hospital clinics, physicians are essentially free agents and thus, although the physician in charge of a clinic may be a strong supporter of your research project, he or she cannot force an individual physician to cooperate. So, in most clinic settings, if you are a research psychologist and you are not directly or immediately contributing to the clinical enterprise, you must be especially aware of the priorities of the clinic staff.

In addition, even though you might be a principal investigator on a large grant, in many ways you are not considered an equal with physicians and other clinical staff who are charged with treating patients. Unless a hospital has obtained some sort of exemption, federal statute (i.e., Health Insurance Portability and Accountability Act) requires that only people with a clinical relationship to a patient may approach them and solicit their participation in research. Thus, the initial contact must be made by a physician, nurse, or some other clinical staff member. As a result, without the endorsement and cooperation of physicians and/or their clinical support staff, the research project will not be possible. They may be interested in your research and see it as valuable, but if they think it will interfere with the delivery of clinical services or somehow harm their patients, they will not agree to it.

Having learned about these concerns over the years, my research colleagues at KCI and I now, before a project even begins, attempt to brief all the clinic physicians on what we are planning to do and why. In this briefing we repeatedly make clear that we understand the first priority in the clinic is treating patients and that nothing should disrupt the flow of patient appointments. However, much more important than these meetings are those with the staff actually responsible for making a hospital clinic run efficiently—that is, the clinic nursing staff. It is they who will determine whether we can (or cannot) reliably collect the data we need. Our project managers spend hours with the clinical nursing staff before any project begins. During this time, they collaboratively work out ways in which we can collect data with minimal or no disruptions to a clinic's operation. Once we feel nursing supervisors are comfortable and familiar with our research staff and the project, then, in collaboration with them, we roll out the project to all the nurses, usually at a breakfast or lunch that we bring to the clinic. We have found that providing such refreshments makes nurses much more receptive to a project, perhaps because others rarely show them this kind of regard. Such groundwork is critical not only for a current project but for future ones as well. We now have relatively little trouble conducting clinic-based research because we have developed a rapport with the clinical nursing staff and a reputation as researchers who understand how clinics work and know how to collect data with little if any impact on clinic flow. Forging research alliances with physicians and other clinical staff requires an understanding of and responsiveness to their priorities, with slow and careful development of their trust that we will not disrupt or challenge these priorities.

WHAT UNIQUE CHALLENGES EXIST WHEN PHYSICIANS ARE PARTICIPANTS IN THE RESEARCH?

The kind of research I and other behavioral researchers do in clinical settings has another important aspect. Physicians and other health professionals are not only our collaborators, they are also often research participants. Their concerns in that role may be different from those as collaborators. A brief example serves to illustrate this point. The first study on health care disparities I ever conducted was in a primary care clinic, where most of the physicians who saw patients were medical residents, many of whom were trained outside the United States. Naively, I gathered them all in one room, presented the study, and handed out informed consent forms. Within a minute or two, one resident stood up, tore the consent form into several pieces, and walked out of the room. He was followed out by most of the other residents. After some discussions I realized that they viewed the study as an evaluation of their performance and were not about to provide some unknown outsider with information that might jeopardize their careers. Eventually, I was able to obtain their consent, but I learned some important lessons.

The most important of these was to make special efforts to understand physicians' and health professionals' initial concerns and actively address these before problems arise. When you are planning a study that involves collecting data on clinical interactions, you must think about who the stakeholders are. When we first began to study racial health care disparities, we considered only Black patients and people from the Black community as stakeholders. This was not in and of itself a mistake. It is critical, especially if you are not a member of a racial or ethnic minority group, that you involve (a) community members concerned about health issues and (b) patients similar to those who will be in the study as early as possible in the development of the research project. You need to consult with them extensively on the development of the research instruments you will be using and any interventions you might be planning. Doing this is simply good research practice because it will increase the validity of your research procedures and hopefully the relevance of your research findings. However, there is another very good reason for doing this. There is too long a history of medical research on Blacks that failed to consider their perspective and, whatever the initial motives of the researchers, did much more harm than good. A researcher who does work on issues that affect the health of minority populations has a moral and ethical obligation to involve them in the planning of the research as important community stakeholders. Like physicians in their clinical practice, the primary concern of a behavioral researcher working with medically underserved and ill-served patients is, "First, do no harm."

Nonetheless, we soon realized that we had missed some important stakeholders: the physicians who participate in the research. Physicians' (and other health professionals') specific concerns and fears about behavioral research projects are usually different from those of their patients, but they are just as real and just as serious. So, just as my research colleagues at KCI and I learned to view patients and members of their community as stakeholders, we learned to also include physicians as separate but equally important stakeholders. Thus, in our most recent large-scale behavioral intervention we engaged the physician stakeholders before any data were collected. We initially met with physicians who were both coinvestigators and potential research participants. These meetings were small focus groups with no more than two or three physicians at a time and began with a presentation of the research goals followed by discussions of their reactions to these goals. Most physicians were not used to being participants, and their initial responses often reflected suspicion of our motives and concern about the impact of the study on their professional evaluations. We addressed these concerns in detail and solicited suggestions about how we might allay these fears. The goal of these conversations was to persuade them that the research was worthwhile and they would not be harmed by the research findings. Part of this process also involved including them in the development of the research intervention and deciding what questions we would ask them and their patients. This served to inform us about what we had missed in the development of the research protocol and measures; at the same time, we were able to assuage some of their concerns about the research. In those cases in which we were successful, the physicians then became advocates who helped to recruit colleagues. In sum, we treated physicians no differently than other stakeholders and sought to address their concerns and earn their trust. As a result, more than 90% of the physicians we approached agreed to participate, and only one dropped out of the study.

CONCLUSION

The title of Robert A. Heinlein's science fiction classic *Stranger in a Strange Land* came to mind as I prepared this chapter and reflected on my journey of discoveries (and surprises) when I moved from a department of psychology to a department of oncology in a medical school. In contrast to my experience, the book actually has a very unhappy ending, when the "stranger" is murdered by a mob. Here, I have sought to provide information that will help research psychologists avoid much less dramatic but still unhappy endings. Researchers from essentially two different academic planets can form professional alliances in which they address common research questions. Research psychologists have the skills and training to contribute meaningfully to medical research projects. However, successful involvement requires an understanding of and respect for differences in training and how one approaches research questions, and, as with any stranger in a strange land, learning the local customs and mores. On a practical level, successful collaborations require identifying what motivates physicians to do research; developing strategies to involve them in your research projects; addressing their concerns about how a research project might impact them and their patients; and recognizing that although physicians may be your professional colleagues, they may also be your research participants. And, just as community-based research requires respect for the opinions and perspectives of community participants, hospital-based research requires respect for the opinions and perspectives of those who deliver clinical services to their patients.

REFERENCES

Albrecht, T. L., Ruckdeschel, J. C., Riddle, D. L., Blanchard, C. G., Penner, L. A., Coovert, M. D., & Quinn, G. (2003). Discussing clinical trials with cancer patients. *Medical Encounter, 17,* 10–12.

Byrd, W. M., & Clayton, L. A. (2001). Race, medicine, and health care in the United States: A historical survey. *JAMA, 93*(3 Suppl.), 11S–34S.

Hagiwara, N., Penner, L. A., Gonzalez, R., Eggly, S., Dovidio, J. F., Gaertner, S. L., . . . Albrecht, T. L. (2013). Racial attitudes, physician–patient talk time ratio, and adherence in racially discordant medical interactions. *Social Science & Medicine, 87,* 123–131. http://dx.doi.org/10.1016/j.socscimed.2013.03.016

Hamel, L. M., Chapman, R., Malloy, M., Eggly, S., Penner, L. A., Shields, A. F., . . . Albrecht, T. L. (2015). Critical shortage of African American medical oncologists in the United States. *Journal of Clinical Oncology, 33,* 3697–3700. http://dx.doi.org/10.1200/JCO.2014.59.2493

Hardeman, R. R., Burgess, D., Phelan, S., Yeazel, M., Nelson, D., & van Ryn, M. (2015). Medical student socio-demographic characteristics and attitudes toward patient centered care: Do race, socioeconomic status and gender matter? A report from the Medical Student CHANGES study. *Patient Education and Counseling, 98,* 350–355. http://dx.doi.org/10.1016/j.pec.2014.11.013

Harper, F. W. K., Goodlett, B. D., Trentacosta, C. J., Albrecht, T. L., Taub, J. W., Phipps, S., & Penner, L. A. (2014). Temperament, personality, and quality of life in pediatric cancer patients. *Journal of Pediatric Psychology, 39,* 459–468. http://dx.doi.org/10.1093/jpepsy/jst141

Jones, J. H. (1993). *Bad blood: The Tuskegee syphilis experiment* (Rev. ed.). New York, NY: The Free Press.

Penner, L. A., Blair, I. V., Albrecht, T. L., & Dovidio, J. F. (2014). Reducing racial healthcare disparities: A social psychological analysis. *Policy Insights from the Behavioral and Brain Sciences, 1,* 204–212. http://dx.doi.org/10.1177/2372732214548430

Penner, L. A., Dovidio, J. F., Edmondson, D., Dailey, R. K., Markova, T., Albrecht, T. L., & Gaertner, S. L. (2009). The experience of discrimination and black-white health disparities in medical care. *Journal of Black Psychology, 35,* 180–203. http://dx.doi.org/10.1177/0095798409333585

Penner, L. A., Dovidio, J. F., Gonzalez, R., Albrecht, T. L., Chapman, R., Foster, T., . . . Eggly, S. (2016). The effects of oncologist implicit racial bias in racially discordant oncology interactions. *Journal of Clinical Oncology, 34,* 2874–2880. http://dx.doi.org/10.1200/JCO.2015.66.3658

Penner, L. A., Eggly, S., Griggs, J. J., Underwood, W., III., Orom, H., & Albrecht, T. L. (2012). Life-threatening disparities: The treatment of Black and White cancer patients. *Journal of Social Issues, 68,* 328–357. http://dx.doi.org/10.1111/j.1540-4560.2012.01751.x

Penner, L. A., Guevarra, D. A., Harper, F. W., Taub, J., Phipps, S., Albrecht, T. L., & Kross, E. (2016). Self-distancing buffers high trait anxious pediatric cancer caregivers against short- and longer-term distress. *Clinical Psychological Science, 4,* 629–640. http://dx.doi.org/10.1177/2167702615602864

Peterson, A. M., Harper, F. W. K., Albrecht, T. L., Taub, J. W., Orom, H., Phipps, S., & Penner, L. A. (2014). Parent caregiver self-efficacy and child reactions to pediatric cancer treatment procedures. *Journal of Pediatric Oncology Nursing, 31,* 18–27. http://dx.doi.org/10.1177/1043454213514792

Smedley, B. D., Stith, A. Y., & Nelson, A. R. (Eds.). (2003). *Unequal treatment: Confronting racial and ethnic disparities in health care.* Washington, DC: National Academies Press.

10

Community-Based Organizations: Enhancing Collaboration and Dissemination of Research

Meg A. Bond and Michelle C. Haynes-Baratz

As psychologists interested in pressing social issues—such as discrimination, poverty, sexual violence, and health disparities—we, like others in our field, are not simply interested in understanding these phenomena for the sake of basic science. We also want our research to identify and promote strategies that can mitigate harmful social conditions and provoke social change. In addition to working with organizations aiming to influence policy and legal decisions (see Chapters 4 and 6, this volume), we often work with organizations that are tackling social justice issues "on the ground" in our local communities. Through working with community-based organizations (CBOs), we have seen firsthand the vital role they play in the health and well-being of communities. We have witnessed how their strong community ties often provide them with nuanced

This project was supported by a grant from The Society for the Psychological Study of Social Issues (SPSSI). SPSSI is a professional association that promotes the application of psychological research to important social issues and to public policy solutions. The research was also supported in part by the University of Massachusetts Lowell Office of the Vice Provost for Research and the University of Massachusetts Lowell Department of Psychology.

http://dx.doi.org/10.1037/0000066-011
Making Research Matter: A Psychologist's Guide to Public Engagement, L. R. Tropp (Editor)

understandings of local problems, the barriers that can be encountered when trying to address them, and the strategies that have (and haven't) worked well within their particular communities.

There are many reasons that we, as academic researchers, might be drawn to partner with CBOs. Sometimes we share a research question (e.g., What service delivery approaches are most effective?), sometimes we work with CBOs to access populations of interest (e.g., How can we best reach groups with specialized needs?), and sometimes the CBOs themselves are the primary focus of our study (e.g., What organizational strategies are most effective for incorporating culturally diverse staff?). In each case, our goals are typically twofold: (a) to understand a psychological phenomenon of interest and (b) to provide information that is useful to both practitioners and scholars.

Nonetheless, there is a long history of distrust of academic researchers within many community settings. Moreover, CBOs are often incredibly taxed in terms of their resources, including human capital, and must triage how to spend their time. Understandably, then, CBOs are unlikely to embrace participation in research if they do not see the benefits to their communities and/or are distrustful of the process. To work effectively with CBOs, we believe it is critical that they (a) trust our intentions and capacity as researchers, (b) believe collaboration will deliver value added to their mission, and (c) have confidence that we will engage them as partners and conduct research "with them" as opposed to "on them."

PRINCIPLES THAT GUIDE OUR WORK

In this chapter, we share thoughts on building positive collaborative relationships with CBOs that can enable researchers to make our work more relevant and useful for promoting social change. We briefly describe one of our recent endeavors to illustrate some of the lessons we've learned. Before we do, however, we want to share a few principles that have guided our work:

- We believe researchers have to earn the privilege of collaborating with CBOs. No depth of academic heft is sufficient to open the doors to an honest and trusting relationship.

- To have successful partnerships, academic researchers must actively—and sincerely—value the wisdom and expertise that community members hold. We are lost before we even begin if we approach our role as an expert who can come in to observe and then draw conclusions without fully appreciating and understanding the local context. Mutual respect and a collaborative spirit—acknowledging the depth of expertise CBOs have to contribute alongside offering the useful skill set and perspective that researchers can bring to the table—are essential.

- Even though traditional research paradigms call for strict protocols, we must often adapt our approach to the unique histories, resources, and needs of each community-based group and organization (Trickett, 2009). Relatedly, we need to respect the fact that CBOs exist within a dynamic environment where the demands and conditions that affect their work are constantly changing. Thus, our work with CBOs often needs to be flexible and resilient and ebb and flow with the forces in their lives (e.g., organizational calendars, fiscal cycles) rather be organized primarily around pressures in researchers' lives (e.g., academic calendars, journal submission deadlines).

- For research findings to really matter to communities, sharing results often involves much more than providing a researcher-derived summary at the end of a project. In our experience, ensuring that our results are useful comes from an iterative, interactive process that allows space for our community partners to participate in the interpretation, distillation, and outlining of implications that emerge from the information we have gathered.

- Finally, no comprehensive checklist of actions will lead CBOs to view researchers as worth their time if we don't approach our work with genuine respect and a strong dose of humility (Harrell & Bond, 2006)—or to quote the title of a classic community psychology article by James Kelly, "It 'taint what you do, it's the way that you do it" (Kelly, 1979). The quality of the working relationship is critical.

It is important to note that the kind of research–community partnership we are describing here has much in common with the principles of participatory action research (PAR). PAR has a rich history and a literature of its own (Lykes, 2017), and an in-depth review is beyond the scope of this chapter. Nonetheless, various PAR strategies have three things in common with one another and with the issues we raise here: (a) a focus on being useful to the community with which one is engaged, (b) employment of multiple methods, and (c) an emphasis on collaboration (see Stoecker, 2013).

A CASE EXAMPLE: THE HEALTHY DIVERSITY PROJECT

As scholars, we are both deeply committed to understanding the dynamics around diversity in the workplace. In our research, we focus on challenges that hinder, and best practices that facilitate, the full inclusion of diverse members into all levels of the organizational hierarchy. Toward this end, one of our research projects involved partnering with community health centers (CHCs) to investigate their workforce diversity dynamics. We describe this project here to illustrate not only the value of partnering with CBOs but also how one might initiate such a collaboration as well as the value of adopting a collaborative stance.

The Healthy Diversity Project was a multiphase project in which we examined the dynamics of recruiting, retaining, and promoting racial and ethnic diversity within CHCs across the Commonwealth of Massachusetts. Several features of CHCs make them a distinctive environment in which to study workforce diversity dynamics. First, they serve an extremely diverse clientele. CHCs are typically located in underserved communities and deliver critical health services to the most needy, irrespective of an individual's income or insurance coverage. As such, they serve patients who have limited resources to obtain health care through traditional channels and often serve multicultural, multiethnic, multilingual communities. Second, given the diversity of their patient population, most organizational leaders are keenly attuned to the need for a diverse workforce. For example, the staff at our local Lowell CHC speak more than 28 languages, including Khmer, Laotian, Spanish, Portuguese, Vietnamese, French, Mandarin, Hindi, and Swahili. The prevalence of health disparities in the United States has been identified as a pressing social issue, and the provision of culturally competent care and increasing diversity among health care providers is recognized as essential to addressing this problem (Smedley, Stitch, & Nelson, 2003; Sullivan Commission, 2004). Last, CHCs are committed to hiring and employing from their local communities. Taken together, these features uniquely poise CHCs to provide insight into the diversity dynamics within organizations whose commitment to diverse staffing is core to their mission.

The social science goals of the Healthy Diversity Project were to learn more about (a) the dynamic challenges of hiring, developing, and promoting a diverse health care workforce; (b) promising practices that have been adopted to address these challenges and what organizational conditions support or hinder the adoption of such practices; and (c) what supports CHCs need to enhance their ability to staff for their diverse patient population. However, equally important, we hoped our research would be directly useful to the CHCs in the study—that is, influence action at the organizational, community, state, and national levels. Further, we sought to distill lessons about diverse staffing that could also be broadly relevant for other types of CBOs.

The Healthy Diversity Project employed, in some regard, very straightforward research methods. We surveyed all 52 independent CHCs in Massachusetts (48% response rate), followed by 10 in-depth interviews with CHC executive directors and directors of human resources. In fact, in a traditional research manuscript, along with details about constructs of interest and variables, these data would provide the crux of our method section. Yet intentional decisions and lengthy discussions with our partners permeated every step of the research process—from defining whom exactly to query to designing a questionnaire and the interview protocol for interpreting the results. It was a labor- and time-intensive commitment, but one that we believe was essential to making our work with CBOs relevant and useful.

ESTABLISHING COLLABORATIONS WITH COMMUNITY-BASED ORGANIZATIONS: WHERE DO I START?

Before the research question can be fully articulated, a tremendous amount of work needs to be done in and with the community. In our view, building these community relationships is not just a strategy for gaining cooperation; these relationships are essential to enabling us to base our work with an appreciation for how the social issues we wish to understand unfold in the real world—that is, how people within the local community context experience them, understand them, and seek to address them. As researchers, we often do not even know the most useful questions without help from someone on the "inside." Genuine, trusting, reciprocal relationships with community partners can be an antidote to arrogantly assuming we know a priori how to frame the research goals, questions, and methods (Kelly, 2006).

In this spirit, for our Healthy Diversity Project, we knew we needed to develop partnerships before we could begin much of anything else. We started with a conversation with the chief executive officer (CEO) of a local CHC—a woman with whom a few members of our team had worked in the past. Growing trusting connections takes time, and our history with her went back at least a decade through joint research projects to survey community health needs, evaluation projects, and student placements at her health center. Shifting to a focus on staffing was in sync with many past conversations. Connections that enable researchers to enhance the impact of their research are not simply people they happen to know in the community, but people who are uniquely connected to networks of influence in the community. Our initial contact was not only the CEO of our local CHC; in addition, she was a well-respected community leader more generally, had previously worked at the Massachusetts State Department of Public Health (DPH), and was highly regarded among CHC leaders throughout the state. She introduced us to a policy expert who became our primary partner at the Massachusetts League of Community Health Centers (Mass League), also a well-respected person with a long history of CHC work and strong connections to the Massachusetts DPH and within the CHC world nationally.

These relationships—through the local CHC and Mass League—facilitated our introduction to a statewide network of CHC human resources (HR) managers, opened doors to CHCs statewide, and provided wise counsel throughout. Also at this early stage, we consulted with other connections at the Massachusetts DPH, talked with representatives of a statewide health training network, and gathered an interdisciplinary project advisory board of community and university people interested in public health issues. The details of what we did and who we talked with are not the main points we want to convey here. Rather, we want to illustrate the importance of understanding and tapping not just people but also networks that can actively shape our work as well as lend it legitimacy through their involvement from the start.

HOW CAN COMMUNITY-BASED ORGANIZATIONS CONTRIBUTE TO PLANNING THE RESEARCH?

In addition to helping us refine our understanding of issues we wish to study, key community stakeholders can educate us about critical actors, introduce us to local lingo, alert us to political undercurrents that we need to surf to gather useful data, and help in building a foundation for receptivity to recommendations that will emerge from our research. To illustrate the point, when we first considered the Healthy Diversity Project, we started with a broad Internet search to get a better sense of how many CHCs there were, where they were located, and how they were structured. One would think this process would be fairly straight-forward, but it turned out to be more complex than we had imagined. It soon became clear that CHCs varied more than we had expected, such as in terms of services offered and in terms of organizational and funding structures. Many operated independently with a special designation as federally qualified health centers, while others operated within hospitals. There was also variability within each of these two structures. Given our research focus, we ended up working only with the independent CHCs. The organizational structure mattered tremendously to our focus in that it influenced the degree to which CHCs were able to dictate their own staffing decisions and broader workplace policies. Thus, even this definition of the prospective sample was informed by preliminary conversations with our community partners. Without our knowledgeable community guides, we could have easily ended up unwittingly lumping apples and oranges together.

Strong relationships with CBOs can also help in refining research tools; continual exchange can keep researchers engaged with and responsive to the local expression of problems. Feedback from our Mass League and local CHC contacts had very practical impacts, such as edits to our survey to ensure that the language we used was accessible and familiar to our respondents. In particular, with survey items that included checklists of responses (with instructions to check all that apply), our partners were essential to ensuring meaningful options and creating a comprehensive list, such as for a question about barriers to taking advantage of training offerings.

They also helped us to shape a data-gathering process that was responsive to the culture and logistics of CHC settings. For example, we were interested in collecting information about the demographic makeup of the workforce. The categories we had initially derived from our research practice turned out to be a mismatch with the categories CHCs regularly use for collecting and reporting demographic information. We initially intended to use categories as captured by census data, yet we learned that CHCs collected data using different categories based on requirements of various funding agencies. Ultimately, we consulted with our lead partners to help us adjust our questions—and survey format—based on what would be most workable for CHCs to report. Although this point may seem somewhat mundane, asking HR managers to report data not at their disposal and/or in a new format would have made for a frustrating experience for our participants, and undoubtedly, fewer would have responded. Ultimately, our data could have been quite sparse and thus unusable. Further, in learning more about reporting frameworks for CHCs vis-à-vis patient demographics, we learned that many CHCs complete a variety of demographic reports each year, each utilizing different formats, and thus one of the recommendations emerging from our research was to urge the Massachusetts DPH to lead an effort to promote a consistent reporting framework.

HOW CAN COLLABORATIONS WITH COMMUNITY-BASED ORGANIZATIONS FACILITATE DATA GATHERING?

Our collaborations with CBOs have also been crucial in determining how to reach populations of interest, identify the most reliable informants, clarify the most pressing questions, develop the best ways to ask these questions, and determine what types of methods will work. Having solid relationships with CBOs can greatly strengthen our ability to shape approaches that are in tune with the lives of the people who are the focus of our research. In addition, when doing community-based research, it is useful to know the history of prior experiences that the CBO and community have had with researchers. Have CBOs and/or local community members felt let down— even burned—by researchers in the past? Have past research partners been helpful and receptive to community input? If researchers have disappointed community members in the past, we need to find ways to ensure (and reassure) that we will not do the same. If past relationships with researchers have been positive, we can ask our CBO partners what they most valued and work to incorporate those qualities in our approach. This history can have a significant impact on our ability to gather reliable, honest, and useful data.

More generally, getting very busy CBO executive directors and HR managers to open their doors for interviews is no easy task. They are extremely busy people, often operating in seriously underresourced environments. Our partners' input about exactly how and when to approach the CHCs across the state helped us avoid naïve mistakes that would have been so easy to make, such as sending a survey during budget crunch times, when annual staff evaluations were in full swing, when many CEOs were out of the office at a statewide conference, or when large agency reports were due. They also helped us identify organic moments when people would already be gathered together and potentially open to discussing research summaries (e.g., at statewide meetings, conferences). In addition, the letters of introduction and sponsorship by our local and Mass League contacts were essential for gaining access to administrators. An executive director is more likely to open the door to another executive director who understands their context and their challenges.

HOW CAN COMMUNITY-BASED ORGANIZATIONS HELP WITH INTERPRETATION OF RESEARCH FINDINGS?

Although in our capacity as researchers we might be inclined to assume that our data speaks for itself, we have to keep in mind that our conclusions are also shaped by our own social location. If we don't recognize this, we run the risk of working from faulty assumptions or failing to incorporate important aspects of participants' lived experience into our analysis. Thus, once data have been collected, researchers can benefit from, once again, engaging CBO partners, to help make sense of research findings and to ensure that researcher interpretations reflect the lived reality that participants intended to share.

To this end, we prepared a report designed to communicate our results to our community partners as well as CHC executives and HR managers in the state and other organizations that influence health and education policy development (Bond, Haynes, Toof, Holmberg, & Reyes Quinteros, 2011b). As we drafted this summary, we worked closely with our primary partner at the Mass League and incorporated her feedback. For example, she reminded us that it was critical to factor in the history of community health in the United States. CHCs grew out of a movement to rethink health in low-income communities to include broader quality-of-life issues (i.e., poverty, housing, food insecurity, access to healthy foods, and access to social services). CHCs are not just another traditional health center that happens to be located in a low-income community— a fact that is connected to organizational commitment to foster diverse staffing. Many of the CHC leaders who are still grounded in the original ideological and idealistic origins are now close to retirement, and some are worried that these social change roots will be forgotten by the next generation. The ongoing reminders from our partners about this important history and its relevance to current challenges led us to incorporate this context in our report. As a result of our in-depth conversations, we reconceptualized several of our interpretations relevant to CHC efforts to groom future leaders.

Also important was getting our partner's input on our recommendations—some of which were more feasible than others and/or needed to be rewritten to acknowledge current political and funding realities. We also went back to the statewide group of HR managers to share the next draft of our results and ask for their input on what recommendations might be missing and/or need recalibrating. In addition, we shared our draft report and got feedback from our initial CEO partner at the local CHC. These people provided useful reality testing, such as reminders that because in health care one cannot leave patients unattended, any recommendations related to staff training have to be coupled with plans for replacement personnel coverage. Each layer of feedback accomplished at least two things: (a) increased our responsiveness to and understanding of the nuances of the phenomenon we were trying to summarize and (b) helped to recruit new partners invested in activating change based on our recommendations.

Our partners also reminded us about how to present results in a manner that could be heard by various audiences. In an academic report, it might be acceptable to level a strong critique of CBOs and the approaches they have adopted to the social issue we study. However, if we want our insights to be adopted by CBOs, we have to think more carefully about how we frame such critiques. For example, some of our interviewees spoke about having a diversity day during which staff members celebrate their culture with coworkers; these events most often revolved around sharing food and cultural traditions. Some managers described these as invaluable for building a sense of community and awareness across different cultures. They were very proud of these efforts. Yet such events were also described by members of minority groups as simplistic representations of their culture, missing the more important issues of values, experiences, and worldviews. Often unintentionally, diversity days can convey that what matters most about various cultures is the food and artifacts, an approach that risks reducing cultural differences to clichés. Further, when all nondominant groups are celebrated together, that tends to highlight their status as different from the White norm, and important differences among—and, just as important, within—racial and ethnic groups receive little attention. To respectfully convey this critique of diversity days, we had to be keenly aware of the possible defensiveness of our audience. Our approach was to acknowledge the events as clearly well intentioned with some potential for community building, yet then to also very directly outline the potential unintended negative consequences. We found it important to avoid suggesting that such events are wrong; instead, we conveyed that they should be reconsidered and/or reconceptualized as only one small part of a more multifaceted approach.

HOW CAN I EFFECTIVELY SHARE
RESEARCH FINDINGS WITH COMMUNITIES?

Throughout this chapter, we have argued that efforts toward relevance start even before the research formally begins. In addition, we have some additional thoughts specific to dissemination, regarding (a) framing the results for different audiences and (b) extending networks for dissemination.

Framing Results for Different Audiences

An academic research report is rarely going to be read from beginning to end by CBO leaders and other community change agents—they are busy people. We need to get to the point more quickly. That is, we need to translate research into usable pointers without the endless caveats that creep into our formal academic writing. We suggest that this is not simply a matter of using simpler language but a matter of framing the presentation of results differently for different audiences. For instance, a focus for CBO managers might address the question "What do effective strategies look like?"; framing for theory development might address the question "What are the complex organizational dynamics that affect the expression of the phenomena of interest?"; and a framing for policy development might be around "What financial and political resources do CBOs need to promote desired changes?" How results are presented is elemental to whether the findings and implications will be useful for each audience and to what types of actions will be considered. Moreover, even within academic or policy circles, different frames might highlight different aspects of the research findings for different outlets.

Two of many possible ways for us to frame the results of our study were around (a) best practices to promote diversity within the CHC workforce or (b) dynamic forces that affect the CHCs' ability to hire and integrate diverse workers at all levels of the organization. One frame basically conveys, "Here are some very specific ideas about strategies CHCs can adopt to diversify," and the other conveys, "Here are dynamic forces that CHCs need to navigate when trying to staff for diversity." Both are arguably practical and can be combined, but they speak to different—albeit overlapping—audiences: The best practices frame is more universally prescriptive, whereas the dynamic forces frame is more contextual and allows for different approaches under different conditions. A list of best practices may be more useful for those needing to advocate for the adoption of a particular strategy; an understanding of dynamic forces that affect success is likely to be more useful for those who are tasked with actually implementing and navigating the bumps encountered during the change process.

Working from a best practices frame, in our primary report for the CHCs we provided recommendations organized around functions such as recruitment and hiring, training, promoting positive work relations, and organizational policies (Bond et al., 2011b). These recommendations were fairly concrete, specific, and actionable steps that individual CHCs, the Mass League, and the Massachusetts DPH could take. In keeping with the CHC philosophy of engaging the local community in the delivery of health services, one of our recommendations suggested that CHCs embrace a grow-your-own approach to fostering diversity—that is, recruiting for diversity that reflects the patient population from within the local community and then making a long-term commitment to employee development to enable those hired at entry level to move up through the ranks. We also advocated for policies and state funding to support a grow-your-own approach, such as increased statewide training resources (e.g., regional structures for training coordination, better systems to inform people of training opportunities), expanded access to formal educational opportunities, and the development of more formalized mentoring programs both locally and statewide. The action recommendations involved changes such as organizational policies that promote access to training, work by statewide networks, priority setting by the Massachusetts DPH, and state policies that would enhance funding for related initiatives.

Working from a dynamic forces frame, we organized results in terms of the issues at multiple levels of analysis that could either enable or hinder CHC efforts to work toward workforce diversity (Haynes, Toof, Holmberg, & Bond, 2012). This alternative framing, which builds upon Lewin's (1935) notion of a force field, is less prescriptive and promotes strategies that account for situational factors and local conditions. This framing can be helpful for organizational leaders trying to understand why it is so difficult to implement standard change strategies in their particular organization by shining light on local forces that can create hurdles. For example, some strategies that emerge from a best practices frame might work in an organization that primarily serves one ethnic or cultural group, such as CHCs in predominantly Latino/a communities, but not in a CHC that serves numerous diverse language and cultural groups. Within the frame of dynamic forces that may inhibit change, we can expand our analysis to include the broader context, such as community development initiatives, policies to address economic instability, and advocacy for more school funding in low-income neighborhoods. The dynamic forces framing can also be more thought-provoking and enrich the work of academics seeking to understand the social ecology of workplace diversity (Bond & Haynes, 2014). However, it can be less useful for legislative policy advocates who may benefit from more precise and targeted recommendations.

Partnering for Dissemination

Once the recommendations are framed and articulated, the process of sharing them is also grounded in partnership—and likely to involve different partnerships for different audiences. For us as researchers, it is useful to think broadly about the various constituencies potentially interested in our work. The CBOs that partner in a research project are an obvious first stop, but it's worth thinking more broadly—locally, regionally, nationally. Who else in the local community has some leverage for making recommended changes? What networks are potential resources in advocating for needed changes (professional networks, national associations, local and national advocacy groups)? In our case, we worked with the Mass League to share results with their office, with a statewide network of CHC HR managers, and with a statewide training network. We sent the report to every CHC in the state—not just to those that participated in interviews. We sent it to elected officials. We joined our community partners in presenting the initiative at the annual policy conference of the National Association of Community Health Centers (Haynes et al., 2012).

One positive outcome was a new partnership between our group, the Mass League, and statewide training advocates to expand partnerships among CHCs, community colleges, and universities to provide more professional development opportunities for diverse community members (Haynes, Bond, Toof, Holmberg, & Shroll, 2015).

Our own professional networks are also important audiences for our work, both within psychology and within other fields. We presented some of our findings at conferences of the American Psychological Association (Bond, Haynes, & Toof, 2011), the Society for Community Research and Action (Bond, Haynes, Toof, Holmberg, & Reyes Quinteros, 2011a), and the Society for the Psychological Study of Social Issues (Bond, Haynes, & Toof, 2014). We also went outside of our discipline and made very helpful connections with other researchers working with CHCs when we presented at the Eastern Sociological Society conference (Haynes, Bond, & Toof, 2013). Conferences attended by professionals who work in CBOs are outlets often not on an academic's radar. Ask the members of the CBOs that you work with where they go for professional development opportunities: What newsletters do they read? What conferences support their work? What types of social media do they access? What agencies fund their projects? What networks provide critical resources for their organization? These entities and outlets would likely be very interested in your research findings. There may also be CBOs with very different missions who face challenges related to your research who could benefit from increased dialogue enabled by your dissemination efforts.

CONCLUSION

If nothing else, we hope that we have convinced you that developing genuinely collaborative relationships with CBOs is critical to making research relevant. Real-world relevance is enhanced by partnerships that permeate all aspects and stages of the research process. No comprehensive checklist of things to do or say can fully communicate the importance of fostering respectful partnerships. Rather, being an effective partner often involves years of relationship building with community members and learning through that process how the partnership can best be nurtured. It involves hard work, yet we have found that the investment is well worth it in terms of both the ways in which such relationships can enrich our understanding of the social issues we are passionate about, and the ways in which these partnerships can open up new avenues for action.

REFERENCES

Bond, M. A., & Haynes, M. C. (2014). Workplace diversity: A social ecological framework and policy implications. *Social Issues and Policy Review, 8*, 167–201. http://dx.doi.org/10.1111/sipr.12005

Bond, M. A., Haynes, M., & Toof, R. A. (2011, August). Setting the stage for policy work: Research with community health centers. In S. Shumaker (Chair), *Research for social justice: SPSSI's commitments to action research and policy relevance.* Symposium for the SPSSI 75th Anniversary Celebration conducted at the American Psychological Association Convention, Washington, DC.

Bond, M. A., Haynes, M., & Toof, R. A. (2014, June). Collaborating with community health centers: Reflections on partnerships for action. In G. Maruyama (Chair), *Bridges and barriers: Fostering community-based research across settings and circumstances.* Symposium conducted at the 10th Biennial Society for the Psychological Study of Social Issues Convention, Portland, OR.

Bond, M. A., Haynes, M., Toof, R. A., Holmberg, M., & Reyes Quinteros, J. (2011a, June). *Empowering settings: Organizational practices that support diversity in community health centers.* Paper presented at the Society for Community Research and Action Conference, Chicago, IL.

Bond, M. A., Haynes, M., Toof, R. A., Holmberg, M., & Reyes Quinteros, J. (2011b). *Healthy diversity: Practices that support diverse staffing in community health centers.* Retrieved from University of Massachusetts Lowell, Center for Women & Work website: https://www.uml.edu/docs/Healthy%20Diversity%20Report_tcm18-49658.pdf

Harrell, S. P., & Bond, M. A. (2006). Listening to diversity stories: Principles for practice in community research and action. *American Journal of Community Psychology, 37*, 293–301. http://dx.doi.org/10.1007/s10464-006-9042-7

Haynes, M. C., Bond, M. A., & Toof, R. A. (2013, March). *Supporting a diverse healthcare workforce through innovative partnerships.* Paper presented at the annual meeting of the Eastern Sociological Society, Boston, MA.

Haynes, M. C., Bond, M. A., Toof, R. A., Holmberg, M. D., & Shroll, T. (2015). Supporting a diverse healthcare workforce through innovative partnerships. In M. Duffy, A. Armenia, & C. Stacey (Eds.), *Caring on the clock: The complexities and contradictions of paid care work* (pp. 263–274). Piscataway, NJ: Rutgers University Press.

Haynes, M. C., Toof, R. A., Holmberg, M. D., & Bond, M. A. (2012). Diversification of the health care workforce: Six research propositions for future research. *The International Journal of Diversity in Organisations, Communities and Nations: Annual Review, 11*(5), 163–174. http://dx.doi.org/10.18848/1447-9532/CGP/v11i05/39044

Haynes, M., Toof, R. A., Holmberg, M., Grigg-Saito, D., Leary, M., & Bond, M. A. (2012, March). *Developing a culturally responsive workforce: Challenges, promising practices, and policy implications.* Workshop for the Policy and Issues Forum of the National Association of Community Health Centers, Washington, DC.

Kelly, J. (1979). 'Taint what you do, it's the way that you do it. *American Journal of Community Psychology, 7,* 244–258.

Kelly, J. (2006). *Becoming ecological: An expedition into community psychology.* http://dx.doi.org/10.1093/acprof:oso/9780195173796.001.0001

Lewin, K. (1935). *A dynamic theory of personality.* New York, NY: McGraw-Hill.

Lykes, M. B. (2017). Community-based and participatory action research: Community psychology collaborations within and across borders. In M. A. Bond, I. Serrano-García, C. B. Keys, & M. Shinn (Eds.), *Handbook of community psychology: Vol. 2. Methods for community research and action for diverse groups and issues* (pp. 43–58). Washington, DC: American Psychological Association.

Smedley, B., Stitch, A. Y., & Nelson, A. R. (Eds.). (2003). *Unequal treatment: Confronting racial and ethnic disparities in health care.* Washington, DC: National Academies Press.

Stoecker, R. (2013). *Research methods for community change: A project-based approach* (2nd ed.). Thousand Oaks, CA: Sage.

Sullivan Commission. (2004). *Missing persons: Minorities in the health professions.* Retrieved from http://health-equity.lib.umd.edu/40/1/Sullivan_Final_Report_000.pdf

Trickett, E. J. (2009). Community psychology: Individuals and interventions in community context. *Annual Review of Psychology, 60,* 395–419. http://dx.doi.org/10.1146/annurev.psych.60.110707.163517

11

Teaching and Mentoring: How to Involve Students in Engaged Scholarship

Jamie Franco-Zamudio and Regina Langhout

As social justice scholars, we typically seek to engage in research and/or service that is of use to specific groups (e.g., community-based organizations), for specific causes (e.g., addressing racism in schools), and that enable students to "be of use" (e.g., Fine & Barreras, 2001). To meet tenure and promotion demands, faculty often find it beneficial to pursue academic goals through the alignment of research, teaching, and service, along the lines of what is known as "engaged scholarship" (Boyer, 1996). This is especially true for faculty at liberal arts colleges, where teaching loads are higher and where teacher–student interactions are emphasized (Boyer, 2016). By identifying projects that simultaneously promote student learning, inform research, and serve community needs, multiple goals are met.

http://dx.doi.org/10.1037/0000066-012
Making Research Matter: A Psychologist's Guide to Public Engagement, L. R. Tropp (Editor)

With limited personal and economic resources, it can be difficult to develop a project that simultaneously enriches students' educational experiences, gives back to the local community in a meaningful way, and assists in meeting professional goals. Have you ever questioned whether it is truly feasible to meet all of the criteria for promotion and tenure or to accomplish all of your professional goals? You are not alone. In a conversation with a colleague in the chemistry department at her small, liberal arts college, Franco-Zamudio realized that this was a question that was not specific to psychology faculty. Her colleague shared that she was meeting her teaching and service goals, but she was finding it difficult to conduct her own experiments in order to meet her scholarship goals. This colleague was teaching a service-learning class in which students were developing hands-on chemistry assignments for use at the local high school. The high school did not have the funding to purchase solutions and materials, so the project was mutually beneficial—the high school students were exposed to an intensive lab experience and the college students were gaining valuable teaching skills. In contrast, Franco-Zamudio was conducting several student-led projects on campus, but did not feel sufficiently connected to the community. In order to assess the benefits of the chemistry students' civic engagement, the two faculty members decided to add a pretest and posttest to the existing service-learning class (see Moely, Mercer, Ilustre, Miron, & McFarland, 2002), which provided data that led to a conference presentation coauthored with students.

In this chapter, we emphasize the value of student engagement and engaged scholarship through a social justice lens. In many instances, students are only exposed to charity-based models of civic engagement, such as volunteering at a soup kitchen (Westheimer & Kahne, 2004a, 2004b). Although charity-based models are important in that they provide services and resources, this type of civic engagement alone does not often lead to the structural change necessary to eliminate specific social inequalities (Nelson & Prilleltensky, 2010). There are other models of civic engagement, sometimes referred to as *social justice civic engagement*, that specifically aim to reduce inequities by changing unfair policies, programs, and procedures (Nelson & Prilleltensky, 2010; Perkins et al., 2007; Westheimer & Kahne, 2004a, 2004b).

The chapter describes social justice civic engagement in relation to faculty motivations, understanding student motivations, understanding community partner motivations, and how we are effectively structuring student engagement opportunities.[1] Throughout the chapter, we as coauthors share our own experiences of engaging students in the community and share some general practices others have used to do so. Irrespective of your motivations, we hope this chapter provides you with some ideas and useful tools to facilitate student collaboration with community partners.

WHAT MOTIVATES FACULTY TO INVOLVE STUDENTS IN COMMUNITY-BASED PROJECTS?

As faculty, many of us are motivated to involve students in community-based projects, because we feel strong ethical obligations to: (a) make university resources available to local communities, and (b) provide opportunities for students to put theory into practice through engagement with the communities in which they (and we) are members. Activities such as experiential learning assignments, service-learning courses, and internships can enable students to learn multiple ways to positively impact communities. Examples might include partnering with organizations to create art projects (e.g., painting murals), developing fundraising plans via social media for grassroots organizations, or promoting science programs in underresourced schools (see Fine & Barreras, 2001). To provide a more concrete example, Langhout taught a class where students conducted survey research that enabled a local family resource center to provide mobile health clinic services to migrant farm workers and their families who previously had minimal or no access to health care. This project provided students with a direct opportunity to benefit the local

---

[1] Additional resources to help you learn more about engaging in community-based work are available through the Community Toolbox website (http://ctb.ku.edu/en/get-started) and the website of the Society for Community Research and Action: Division of Community Psychology (Division 27 of the American Psychological Association; http://www.scra27.org).

community, which was especially meaningful to students with ties to migrant farm labor communities.

Engaging students in community-based projects might also serve to meet our teaching goals or learning objectives. By participating in experiential learning, students often gain new insight while developing transferable skills. As a result, they often become more aware of specific social issues or types of injustice and feel a responsibility to act to remedy the injustice (Wauhkonen, 2012). Social justice–based learning experiences and internships might even lead students to change their major or clarify their career goals (Wauhkonen, 2012), while, at the same time enhancing their interpersonal skills (Smirles, 2011).

Working alongside students in community settings can provide faculty with not only ideas for research projects and teaching modules but also new insights and ways of thinking. In particular, community-based projects have the potential to shift the ways in which academics understand and define the problems we study. Although people in the academy, policymakers, and the media often retain sole control over the definitions of social problems, partnering with a community or organization can bring new insights to light (Rappaport, 1990). For example, in a research project carried out in one of Langhout's classes, students talked with people who were not housed, initially asking them about questions that should be included in a survey of unhoused people. One man the students spoke to was adamant that a question be included as to whether or not people were homeless by choice (to combat the narrative that people are homeless because they choose to be). The result of including that question in the survey was that, out of the hundreds of completed questionnaires, only one person marked that they were homeless "by choice." This example illustrates the point that, there are new and different ways to conceive of social problems that can result from student community involvement, often resulting in better research for faculty (Fine, 2006).

As we mentioned earlier, there are also practical reasons why faculty might be motivated to engage students in community-based projects. At academic institutions where teaching loads are high and class sizes are relatively small, course components that include engaged scholarship can be reported on tenure and promotion materials as evidence of teaching excellence, service to the community and students, and—if the project is aligned with research—evidence of scholarship.[2] To provide an illustrative example, Franco-Zamudio is employed at a small college with a high teaching load. Experiential-learning coursework was developed with the intention of meeting teaching and service goals. One specific assignment, where a training workshop for a local nonprofit was developed and facilitated, provided students with an education experience and provided the community organization with a valuable resource. In addition, the assignment enabled faculty to network and develop relationships that would later result in a collaborative research project.

WHAT MOTIVATES STUDENTS TO BECOME INVOLVED IN COMMUNITY-BASED PROJECTS?

Beyond gaining valuable research and professional skills, students are often motivated to participate in community-based work because of their identities and life experiences. Some are members of a community, or have close ties to a community, for which they have a desire or feel a moral obligation to serve. Additionally, students can be drawn to particular field sites due to their own collective identities—whether based on religious, gender, ethnicity, race, nationality, political ideology, or other affiliations. By participating in activities alongside those with a shared identity or purpose, students might feel a sense of affirmation related to that identity and/or a greater sense of connection to the community. For example, students of color have told us that engagement with communities similar to their background can make it easier to navigate predominantly or historically White universities as well as to remind them that their unique perspective and contributions will enable discovery of further knowledge.

Students sometimes report that they participate in community-based projects simply because they need to fulfill a course or major requirement.

---

[2] In particular, the Community-Campus Partnerships for Health website offers useful information on how to document community-engaged scholarship and prepare strong portfolios for tenure and promotion (see https://ccph.memberclicks.net).

If you find yourself teaching students who are less motivated to engage in community-based work, you can point out the broader benefits of experiential learning, such as opportunities to integrate theory and practice into real-world settings. You can also remind students that they can develop and strengthen many transferrable professional skills through such experiences. These skills range from networking to team building to effective communication, which have virtually universal applicability to the organizational contexts in which students might work after graduation.

HOW CAN I DEVELOP EFFECTIVE COLLABORATIONS WITH COMMUNITY-BASED ORGANIZATIONS?

Academics and academic institutions can often provide community-based organizations with additional resources and connections that can help them expand services or resources for their clients, and to meet other organizational objectives (Bystydzienski & Schacht, 2001). Community partners might also seek academics' support in addressing urgent issues that have come to the forefront of local or national politics or support in an effort to create long-term, permanent social change (Wittig, 1996). Regardless of the specific motivations involved, it can be quite helpful to discuss your own and your community collaborator's motivations when establishing a partnership. This will help clarify each party's needs and expectations and help assess if those needs and goals can be met through working together.

Before any collaboration begins, however, one must find willing and compatible community partners. If you are unsure of how to begin, first investigate whether your campus has a community engagement center or an internship office, or whether your town has a volunteer center. These offices can be great resources for faculty new to student engagement, or to a faculty member new to a specific location, as those resources tend to have extensive networks of contacts across a range of organizations. If no such resources exist, we recommend having students research local organizations as part of their relevant coursework. They can read the local paper, attend city council meetings and public hearings, or interview members of the local school board or county board of supervisors to begin a community mapping exercise (see, e.g., Lykes's, 2010, community mapping exercise). Such explorations can provide the students (and you) with important information on how local government operates, which issues are viewed as important (and by whom), who attends meetings and what issues they raise, and, more generally, how the community is viewed by local officials and civic leaders. Some partnerships have developed as the result of students' attending public meetings. More broadly, however, having students pursue these strategies is a fairly low-risk way to foster their community engagement in that it often piques their interest and provides you with important contextual information that can serve as a foundation for developing future community engagement projects.

We are often inclined to pursue collaborations with community partners because they share a commitment to issues that match our research interests and expertise, or because they would allow students to learn about the strengths and gifts of people who are different from them in some way (e.g., age, ability, social class). However, students may also have ideas about locations for their community engagement. Sometimes students are already active within a community; yet, at times, the student involvement is not viewed as "community engagement" or "service learning" because their activities are not affiliated with an established organization (e.g., watching children after school, providing homework help). In such cases, you might be able to work with students to identify an organization that is engaged in related work, and to specify a research question or an applied objective for this work, so they can parlay their skills and experience into a community-based project for which they can receive academic credit. As a general principle, it is useful to think about the types of organizations and activities that would be most appropriate for any community engagement projects you commence or supervise, so that these parameters can be communicated to and discussed with both your students and the sponsoring organization.

On a practical level, it is important to choose organizations that have the capacity to supervise students, and are able to work with them within the time frame that you have determined—whether that is for a weekend, a school term, or an academic year. We recommend having a conversation with the organization about the focus and content of the university-based structure (e.g., course, internship, program sponsored by community engagement center), your experiential goals for the students, and how your students might contribute to the activities of the organization. Is it appropriate for the student to spend more than half their time photo-copying and filing? If not, say so. If the organization has special require-ments for students (e.g., they must undergo a background check, bilingual English and Spanish speaker preferred), then that should be made clear. As part of this process, we recommend that you both share your relevant materials (e.g., course syllabus) and ask the organization to write a brief statement about the placement and expectations of the students during the community engagement project.

If a longer term placement is involved (i.e., more than a few weeks), let the organization know that you would like a representative or volunteer supervisor to work with the students in the first week of the field place-ment in order to develop a community contract. The goal of the contract is to make explicit the expectations, processes, goals, and/or outcomes that are associated with this community-based work—which should enhance the experience for the students and the organization. This document should cover the scope of the work, who is involved and in what capacity, how these individuals should communicate with one another, when the work will be done, and how to deal with any conflicts that arise. The con-tract should be signed by the students and organizational representatives, and should be viewed as binding by both groups.

When developing communication strategies and plans for success-ful partnerships, in order to maintain cooperative dialogue and shared practical action, you might include agreed-upon principles similar to those outlined in the framework of transcommunality (Childs, 2003). An important aspect of transcommunality is that it validates and values all identities, and stresses "mutual recognition" between groups (Childs, 2003). As such, differences are not ignored but perceived as sources from which alliances draw their greatest strength and ingenuity. Without first acknowledging differences and creating mutually beneficial goals and strategies, interactions between academics and community partners might appear insincere, which hinders trust. It can be especially important to articulate differences in perspective or potential problems early in the partnership. By recognizing the reality of intergroup differences, partners can be better equipped to work out compromises to bridge gaps, through both talking and listening, and through being sensitive to the interests, concerns, fears, and hopes of all parties involved (Childs, 2003).

It is also possible for partners with different constituencies to collaborate on joint projects, while maintaining their own separate identities and organizational goals. For example, student volunteers working at a community-based women's center might join students working at a homeless shelter to advocate for spaces for women and children fleeing their homes due to family violence. Those students might also invite student interns at a law firm to assist them in locating legal services or resources. Although each entity has a different overarching goal or mission, and students are working to fulfill the obligations of the community organization with which they have established an agreement, together they might engage in temporary projects aimed at shared practical action.

HOW CAN I EFFECTIVELY PREPARE STUDENTS FOR COLLABORATIONS WITH COMMUNITY-BASED ORGANIZATIONS?

No matter what kind of community-based work might be involved, it is important to set explicit and clear expectations for student conduct from the outset. We often inform students about the history of "town–gown" relations and communicate that the relationships they develop with community partners are ultimately more important than their individual performance, because these relationships happen within the context of historical and often tense relations between town and university. Their grade, recommendation letter, or whatever external motivator might be connected to students' involvement, has implications only for them. This is often sobering for students to hear. However, it is vital to remind them that staff at the community site often rely on the work of university students and that community–university relations are built upon shared trust and the understanding that certain outcomes will be accomplished.

When selecting undergraduates for community-based projects, we find it useful to require an application and an interview. We recommend recruiting students outside of any single major in order to diversify perspectives. Interview questions should assess whether students are comfortable with ambiguity, if they have prior experience with the community or population with which they would be working, as well as their prior research experience, their ability to engage in teamwork, and their leadership skills. It is important to select students with a diverse set of skills who you think will work well together.

We strongly recommend having students work in groups at each site, and when possible, pairing students with complementary skill sets. Working collaboratively with other students enables them to learn from each other, making them more effective at their job or task. Also, we recommend having students develop another contract among themselves, so that they know who will take on what roles, how they will communicate with each other, and how they will deal with conflict. Subsequently, if and when the students come to you out of frustration with their group, you can ask them about their contract and if they have followed their preestablished agreements. This often helps the group to regulate and resolve conflicts internally.

Even with these procedures and guidelines in place, occasionally a student is not yet ready for a specific community placement, or the community organization is not ready for students. It might be that the student is having difficulties with following through, there is a bad fit between the community partner and the student, the organization treats the student in ways the student deems as discriminatory, or there is some skill that the student lacks and is struggling to develop. In some cases, you may decide that the placement should not continue. It is then important to have a backup plan to specify what alternate work the student can complete to receive academic credit or other forms of recognition for their work; for example, a literature review–style paper might help the student to learn more about topics relevant to the community placement or better understand the challenges that they have experienced within the community placement.

HOW MIGHT STUDENT ENGAGEMENT ACTIVITIES BE STRUCTURED?

Quite often, student engagement activities are structured as part of an undergraduate class for which students can receive course credit. When outlining the syllabus for the class, we suggest including time for group work and for students to receive feedback from you and other students. We have found that, especially for first-generation college students and students who have outside jobs/other family-related commitments, a structure that works well is to have the class meet three times a week. One day each week is dedicated to group work (where the instructor rotates among groups), and 2 days each week are devoted to readings and other course content. On group work days, we recommend that the faculty member check in with all groups in terms of their internal group process, how their community engagement projects are progressing, and whether they feel they have the skills to manage their community projects appropriately. Skills that are sometimes at issue include knowing how to work effectively with diverse populations, as well as the students' ability to overcome assumptions about specific people or communities they may encounter.

Structures Involving Coursework

Depending upon the needs of the community partner, there are many different projects that students might choose to undertake for which they can receive course credit. Fine and Barreras (2001) suggested numerous ideas, such as creating curricula for local schools and developing art or media projects that disseminate research findings to a broader audience. Inspired by these authors, Franco-Zamudio has considered the types of projects that could simultaneously meet course learning objectives and the needs of community sites. In one class on organizational psychology, students work with a specific community organization to develop a semester-long project intended to meet their needs. To be consistent with the goals of an organizational psychology course, students are instructed to identify a project that would help the organization to function better (rather than seeking to improve upon the services they provide to clients). The staff at the community organization indicate where they have the greatest need, and over the course of the semester, students learn to create job descriptions, training programs, assessment tools, and informational workshops that would enhance the functioning of the organization. At times, community organizations request that students use specific methodologies or technology that are not covered in class. In cases like these, we invite local experts to campus to train students. Some skills are requested so often (e.g., fundraising event planning) that we offer a short-term training program via a one-credit course for students from this class and across campus.

In addition to other projects and assignments, encouraging students to complete oral or written reflections on their community-based interactions can help them understand the scope and impact of the work they have conducted at a particular field site. Additionally, it may inspire critical thinking, facilitate meaning, instill a sense of social responsibility, and/or provide closure to a project. Effective reflections typically have a specific outcome in mind (e.g., teambuilding or improved critical thinking) and occur before, during, or after the community experience. Reflections may be written individually or conducted in dyads or groups, and they might be structured as journal prompts, roundtable discussions, or creative outputs.[3]

Structures Involving Research

In addition, you and your students may be interested in pursuing community-based projects connected to your programmatic line of research. The most sustainable model we have followed is the "educational pyramid model" (Seidman & Rappaport, 1974). In this model, or

---

[3] See, for example, the Northwest Service Academy's (n.d.) Service Reflection Toolkit (http://www.dartmouth.edu/~tucker/docs/service/reflection_tools.pdf).

in an adapted version, the professor supervises PhD-level or advanced undergraduate students, who then supervise more novice undergraduates as research assistants. The professor meets weekly with the supervising students (either PhD level or advanced undergraduate) to check in and ensure they get the support they need to supervise their research assistants, and the professor also meets with the research assistants as needed to ensure they have the theoretical foundation and data collection skills needed for the project. Meetings with the professor become less frequent as research assistants gain skills and as supervising students become more adept at supervision.

When recruiting students to work on community-based research, we require a multiterm commitment. Indeed, a lot of time and energy go into training undergraduate research assistants and relationships need to be developed within the community. For this reason, it is important to have a steady and stable group of undergraduates who are committed to the research project over multiple semesters or quarters. For longer term projects, we encourage choosing at least one student who can work on the project for more than one academic year; this will ensure consistency and help with training new research assistants the following year. When we bring in new students to our projects, we scaffold information carefully, being explicit about what to wear, how to interact with the community, and what kinds of conversations are not appropriate. Over time, we have consolidated much of this information into a "handbook," which continues to be updated as the project evolves. Of course, we also provide students with a strong foundation in theory underlying the research project through readings, information on how to collect and analyze data, and opportunities to process their community experiences along the way. Giving students a solid grounding in the literature will help them not jump to conclusions about the research. But the students still may need support in learning the difference between knowing something anecdotally and knowing it empirically. For example, we have had students return to the university after their first 2-hour session at a community placement, speaking with great conviction and conclusiveness about aspects of the setting that need to change. It is important to support this earnestness but at the same time to facilitate a discussion about what we can really know about a place after a 2-hour visit and what additional information we might seek to learn during subsequent visits.

For those undergraduates who demonstrate additional initiative, we often offer opportunities to conduct a senior thesis project grounded in the community-based research. We work with them to carve out a project that is connected to our programmatic line of research but that can be distinctively theirs. For example, they might pose a unique research question that you have not addressed in the community setting but that is connected to your ongoing data collection and could, therefore, be examined relatively easily. This often requires students to craft a 2- to 3-page proposal outlining their ideal research goals, followed by some negotiation with you and the community organization, as is the case with many types of research. In some instances, such as when students demonstrate sustained commitment to the work and uncover interesting findings, we have also encouraged undergraduates to present their research at conferences (e.g., Bowen, 2013; Mitchell, 2003) and/or to copublish research articles with us as faculty supervisors (e.g., Kohfeldt, Bowen, & Langhout, 2016; Langhout & Mitchell, 2008).

Other Structures for Student Engagement

There are other structures you might consider for student engagement, including the possibilities of working with student volunteers or with students who take on short-term consulting roles. Some students may indicate a preference to volunteer for a placement, rather than use a structure you have created (e.g., a set of requirements for course credit). Generally, we would not recommend allowing students to participate in a community-based project unless there is an accountability structure in place. Langhout previously agreed to allow some students to participate in volunteer work on projects, and too many times students got busy with their own school work, jobs, or other aspects of life, and the volunteer work was unfulfilled. Thus, we highly recommend having accountability structures in place for all students connected to you who wish to engage community-based projects.

Additionally, although students are often interested in volunteer opportunities or unpaid internships to gain experience, not all students can afford to participate in community-based activities without some form of compensation. Thus, some students may be recruited to assist faculty in consulting for short-term community-based projects (e.g., a training workshop, a needs assessment), for which students might receive monetary payment for the work instead of academic credit. Other students might engage in the work to strengthen their resumes, or they might use the project for a presentation at a research conference. Additionally, on smaller campuses, students tend to have few opportunities to develop certain skills that would make them more competitive on the job market, thereby making these opportunities for short-term consulting projects especially attractive.

CONCLUDING THOUGHTS

Through our experiences, we have discovered that there is no one best practice for engaging students in community work. It takes time (and a bit of trial and error) to determine what will work best for you and your students. Our advice?

- Start with projects or assignments that can be added to what you are already doing in your coursework and research.
- Connect with community partners by attending local workshops, fundraisers, and networking events.
- Search for ways to align teaching, research, and service as you outline your annual goals.

And last, but not least:

- Don't wait until you get tenure to do community-engaged work.

As scholar–activists committed to social justice, we found it impossible to heed the advice of some, which was to wait until after tenure to engage in community-based work. For us, it was important to pursue the combination of research, teaching, and service that motivated and inspired us, so we began to involve students in community-based projects as soon as we could. If this is the work that drives you, then we invite and encourage you to follow your convictions and embrace the learning that comes from the challenges and accomplishments along the way.

REFERENCES

Bowen, A. (2013, June). Mural creation as a context of intersectional identity expression. In J. M. Silva (Chair), *Praxis: Moving into action*. Symposium conducted at the Society for Community Research and Action, Miami, FL.

Boyer, E. L. (1996). The scholarship of engagement. *Journal of Higher Education Outreach and Engagement, 1*(1), 11–20.

Boyer, E. L. (2016). *Scholarship reconsidered* (Expanded ed.). San Francisco, CA: Jossey-Bass.

Bystydzienski, J. M., & Schacht, S. P. (2001). Introduction. In J. M. Bystydzienski & S. P. Schacht (Eds.), *Forging radical alliances across difference: Coalition politics for the new millennium*. Lanham, MD: Rowman & Littlefield.

Childs, J. B. (2003). *Transcommunality: From the politics of conversion to the ethics of respect*. Philadelphia, PA: Temple University Press.

Fine, M. (2006). Bearing witness: Methods for researching oppression and resistance—A textbook for critical research. *Social Justice Research, 19*, 83–108.

Fine, M., & Barreras, R. (2001). To be of use. *Analyses of Social Issues and Public Policy, 1*, 175–182. http://dx.doi.org/10.1111/1530-2415.00012

Kohfeldt, D., Bowen, A. R., & Langhout, R. D. (2016). "They think kids are stupid": yPAR and confrontations with institutionalized power as contexts for children's identity work. *Revista Puertorriqueña de Psicología, 27*, 276–291.

Langhout, R. D., & Mitchell, C. A. (2008). Engaging contexts: Drawing the link between student and teacher experiences of the hidden curriculum. *Journal of Community & Applied Social Psychology, 18*, 593–614. http://dx.doi.org/10.1002/casp.974

Lykes, M. B. (2010). *PY 912: Participatory action research: Gender, race, and power guidelines for information gathering exercise or community mapping*. Retrieved from https://www2.bc.edu/brinton-lykes/pdf/INFOGATHER_2010.pdf

Mitchell, C. (2003, June). Disciplining discourse: How classroom discipline is mediated by gender and race. In R. D. Langhout (Chair), *Listening to voices in silencing contexts*. Symposium conducted at the meeting for the Society for Community Research and Action, Las Vegas, NV.

Moely, B. E., Mercer, S. H., Ilustre, V., Miron, D., & McFarland, M. (2002). Psychometric properties and correlates of the civic attitudes and skills questionnaire

(CASQ): A measure of students' attitudes related to service-learning. *Michigan Journal of Community Service Learning, 8*(2), 15–26.

Nelson, G., & Prilleltensky, I. (Eds.). (2010). *Community psychology: In pursuit of liberation and well-being* (2nd ed.). New York, NY: Palgrave Macmillan.

Northwest Service Academy. (n.d.). Service reflection toolkit. Retrieved from http://www.dartmouth.edu/~tucker/docs/service/reflection_tools.pdf

Perkins, D. D., Bess, K. D., Cooper, D. G., Jones, D. L., Armstead, T., & Speer, P. W. (2007). Community organizational learning: Case studies illustrating a three-dimensional model of levels and orders of change. *Journal of Community Psychology, 35,* 303–328. http://dx.doi.org/10.1002/jcop.20150

Rappaport, J. (1990). Research methods and the empowerment social agenda. In P. Tolan, C. Keys, F. Chertok, & L. A. Jason (Eds.), *Researching community psychology: Issues of theory and methods* (pp. 51–63). http://dx.doi.org/10.1037/10073-005

Seidman, E., & Rappaport, J. (1974). The educational pyramid: A paradigm for training, research, and manpower utilization in community psychology. *American Journal of Community Psychology, 2,* 119–130. http://dx.doi.org/10.1007/BF00878039

Smirles, K. E. (2011). Service learning in a Psychology of Women course: Transforming students and the community. *Psychology of Women Quarterly, 35,* 331–334. http://dx.doi.org/10.1177/0361684311403660

Wauhkonen, R. (2012, Spring). Experiential learning and the attainment of common general education goals. *The Journal of Pedagogy, Pluralism, and Practice, 4*(4), 6. Retrieved from http://www.lesley.edu/journal-pedagogy-pluralism-practice/robert-wauhkonen/experiential-learning-education-goals/

Westheimer, J., & Kahne, J. (2004a). Educating the "good" citizen: Political choices and pedagogical goals. *PS: Political Science & Politics, 37,* 241–247. http://dx.doi.org/10.1017/S1049096504004160

Westheimer, J., & Kahne, J. (2004b). What kind of citizen? The politics of educating for democracy. *American Educational Research Journal, 41,* 237–269. http://dx.doi.org/10.3102/00028312041002237

Wittig, M. A. (1996). An introduction to social psychological perspectives on grassroots organizing. *Journal of Social Issues, 52,* 3–14. http://dx.doi.org/10.1111/j.1540-4560.1996.tb01358.x

12

Where Have We Been, Where Are We Now, and Where Should We Be? Linking Engagement to Scholarship

John F. Dovidio

Scholars, particularly junior scholars, are often advised against engaging in activities to address social problems because it is believed that these efforts will distract them from pursuing theory-driven research. Indeed, there is limited time to attain the scholarly achievements, as well as excellence in teaching plus service, that are typically expected for tenure and promotion in colleges and universities. Nevertheless, practical applications to address important social problems can stimulate, inform, and enhance scholarship. Practical applications can help us gain a deeper understanding of the processes, influences, and outcomes that we aspire to study in our research.

Kurt Lewin, a noted scholar who has had a profound influence on the field of social psychology, is widely recognized for encouraging researchers to field test their ideas and apply the findings to address social problems (Lewin, 1946). His studies of leadership, attitudes, consumer behavior, and

http://dx.doi.org/10.1037/0000066-013
Making Research Matter: A Psychologist's Guide to Public Engagement, L. R. Tropp (Editor)

social action provide outstanding and enduring examples of the ways in which psychological insights can be applied to promote socially valued behavior. Perhaps, as a consequence, many contemporary psychologists interpret his encouragement for social engagement as a call primarily to apply social psychological research to practical issues. However, Lewin's guidance went far beyond that. Lewin also emphasized the reciprocal value of research and application; not only can theory inform application, but our engagement beyond the laboratory can also inform psychological science in critical ways.

This chapter discusses the value engagement in applied settings has for the science of psychology. This is an opportunity for us to reflect on the current state of our field, to look back to the foundation on which it was built, and to look toward its possible growth in the future. First, I consider factors that may inhibit researchers' involvement in engaged research. Second, I explore the variety of valuable contributions that engaged research can make toward promoting positive change in our society. Finally, the chapter highlights the many ways in which engaged research can make psychologists' science better.

IF ENGAGED RESEARCH IS SO IMPORTANT, WHY ISN'T EVERYBODY DOING IT?

While the idea of testing social psychological theory in applied settings is widely accepted in principle, it represents only a small proportion of current social psychology research (Paluck & Cialdini, 2014). Part of the reason is that research in applied field settings is more methodologically challenging than are studies with convenience samples in psychology laboratories or, increasingly, in online studies with opt-in participant pools (e.g., MTurk; see Buhrmester, Kwang, & Gosling, 2011). However, I believe that the reluctance to embrace field and applied research is not simply due to logistical obstacles but instead is embedded, at least in part, in the politics of our field.

Psychology—and social psychology in particular—has long been a tenuous science. It represents a gateway bridging microlevels of analysis (e.g., brain imaging drawing on techniques from human neuroscience) with macrolevels of analysis (e.g., structural and ideological processes, drawing from work in political science and sociology). Compared with other social sciences, we as psychologists make a "distinctive contribution by explaining the links between the individual and system level of analysis" (Pettigrew, 1988, p. 207). However, our strong and unique emphasis on links between the individual and the social context has raised questions about whether we can identify the kinds of invariant relationships that characterize work in the physical and biological sciences. Indeed, in a critique titled "Social Psychology as History," Gergen (1973) questioned whether social psychology should even be considered a science. Gergen argued that social context changes as a function of political, economic, and historical events, and, thus, our research findings are limited in their generalizability by time and place. Moreover, dissemination of psychological research can accelerate social change in ways that can challenge the validity of previous social psychological findings in more contemporary contexts. In other words, social psychology may perpetually "be chasing its tail."

The study of racial prejudice in the United States illustrates how psychological research can help address an immediate social problem but may also change the phenomenon (i.e., prejudice) in ways that require new theory, research, and interventions to further combat it. In particular, historically, the racial prejudice of White Americans was openly expressed, and this bias blatantly limited opportunities for Black Americans. Psychological research in the 1950s and 1960s called attention to the profoundly negative consequences of traditional racial policies (e.g., segregation) on Blacks and enhanced public recognition that this biased treatment and the attitudes that fueled it were unjust (Dovidio, 2001). Influenced by social norms that condemned racial bias and emphasized the principle of egalitarianism, the civil rights legislation of the 1960s made many of these traditional racial practices illegal.

By the end of the 1970s, however, psychologists recognized a significant change in the way Whites displayed bias. Although Whites typically did not overtly express racial prejudice or directly display racial discrimination, they did discriminate against Blacks indirectly. That is, they discriminated primarily when they could justify negative treatment of Blacks ostensibly on the basis of some factor other than race (e.g., modern racism, symbolic racism, aversive racism; for a review, see Dovidio, Gaertner, & Pearson, 2017). For instance, Whites tended to emphasize a weak aspect of a job applicant's credentials in employment decisions when denying a person employment, but they did so more when the applicant was Black than when the applicant was White.

Furthermore, to better understand subtle discrimination, psychologists developed new techniques to uncover hidden bias. One of the most popular of these techniques is a response-latency measure, the Implicit Association Test (IAT; Greenwald, Poehlman, Uhlmann, & Banaji, 2009). Research using the IAT has revealed how even Whites who consciously endorse egalitarian values and genuinely disavow personal racial prejudice may continue to harbor unconscious (implicit) negative racial attitudes and stereotypes. These implicit biases operate outside of awareness to produce unintentional unfair treatment of Blacks.

Traditionally, legal standards required that conscious intent of bias be demonstrated for a successful prosecution of racial discrimination; this requirement limited the effectiveness of the law in combating subtle bias motivated by unconscious prejudice. However, informed by psychological research, the courts expanded the criteria to recognize the role of implicit bias and the ways in which subtle discrimination can occur (Greenwald & Krieger, 2006). Nevertheless, as we have seen repeatedly over time, when research identifies new types of bias and develops interventions to address them, bias can emerge in even newer forms, requiring additional theories, methods, and strategies to deal with them. As Gergen (1973) suggested, our findings can actually change the nature of phenomenon that we are studying, which limits our ability to draw the kinds of stable, generalizable conclusions that are highly valued in the physical and biological sciences.

Such concerns about the scientific standing of social psychology have led scholars in this area to focus more narrowly on tightly controlled research within laboratory settings. This paradigm shift from the period in which Lewin's work was so influential has had an enduring influence on the field. Currently, our primary standard for evaluating the quality of research encompasses issues of internal validity—the ability to draw cause-and-effect inferences—whereas external validity—the ability to generalize findings to and apply them to different contexts—is relegated to a secondary status, if it is at all considered as a criterion for scholarly publication. This shift to tightly controlled experiments with limited attention to the work's external validity has had consequences for our field's reputation, including raising significant questions about its societal relevance and the importance of its findings (Rodin, 1985).

It is worthwhile for us to revisit the value of field research as an integral component in "full-cycle social psychology" (Cialdini, 1980). Cialdini (1980) advocated for research programs that were grounded in strong theory development and testing, including rigorous laboratory research that could demonstrate internally valid effects and illuminate underlying mechanisms, complemented by applied research in field settings to assess how the phenomena of interest operate in more naturalistic settings. This approach not only tests the robustness and generalizability of laboratory research findings but also can help identify influences that may moderate how these processes operate more broadly. But as Cialdini (2009b) more recently acknowledged, the promise of full-cycle social psychology has not been fulfilled in current practice.

The most recent crisis in psychology, the replicability crisis (Simmons, Nelson, & Simonsohn, 2011), will likely rekindle interest in field research, potentially as a component of full-cycle social psychology. The replicability crisis involves widespread concerns about whether findings obtained through traditional scientific practices can be obtained reliably and questions the validity of psychology research (Open Science Collaboration, 2015). The replicability crisis has its roots in the motivation of individual researchers to gain scholarly and public recognition and of the field, more generally, to distinguish itself scientifically. Scholarly reputations in our field are built on publishing works that are cited by our professional colleagues, that receive broad interest in the media, and attract funding from granting agencies. Success in doing so, which leads to more publishing opportunities and grants, is commonly measured by citation impact (e.g., one's h-index). Thus, we as researchers value the attention colleagues are giving to our work. In part as a response to the growing criticism of the "commonsense" findings of psychology—and of social psychology in particular—our field has attempted to promote its scientific standing with clever methodologies and counterintuitive findings.

However, as consumers are often warned, if something sounds too good to be true, it may not be true. Some of the most intriguing titles and findings, such as "Racial Biases in Legal Decisions Are Reduced by a Justice Focus" (Lammers & Stapel, 2011), "The Secret Life of Emotions" (Ruys & Stapel, 2008), and "When Contact Changes Minds: An Experiment on Transmission of Support for Gay Equality" (LaCour & Green, 2014), published in leading journals, turned out to be based on falsified or unverified data. Ultimately, these papers were retracted by their authors. Fortunately, such cases, which also occur in other scientific disciplines, appear to be limited. But these instances are suggestive of a larger and more common problem in our discipline: namely, the desire to identify and publish counterintuitive findings, which encouraged the adoption of research practices that inflated the likelihood of "false positive" findings involving the rejection of the null hypothesis, when the null hypothesis is actually true (a Type I error). These questionable research practices include (a) reporting only a subset of variables that show the predicted effects, while failing to disclose other key variables that do not show supportive results; (b) providing information only about some of the experimental conditions that were included in the study, that is, the ones that produced effects most consistent with the predictions; and (c) revising the predictions and the rationale to match unanticipated results.

We are now at a critical moment in the history of our field, a moment in which we can take stock and recognize that the dichotomy between rigorous science and engaged research is a false one. Maner (2016) recently argued that field research can play an important role in ensuring the replicability and robustness of social psychological findings. He noted that field research is typically characterized by features that enhance the replicability of findings, such as (a) diverse participant populations, (b) less control over extraneous variables, (c) a focus on behavioral outcomes, and (d) research outcomes that may be informative even if specifically predicted results are not obtained. Thus, testing the implications of psychological theory in field settings can substantially increase confidence in its validity—both internal and external validity. Not only can this directly benefit researchers in pursuit of knowledge, but also it can improve the stature of the field by demonstrating the veracity of the findings and the practical impact and value of the work.

In sum, the dominant, and often narrow, focus on internal validity with limited attention to issues of external validity has contributed to a series of crises that have threatened the scientific standing and integrity of our field. In this context, the "crises" we have faced over the past 50 years, including the recent "replicability crisis," reaffirm the value of scholarly engagement to enhance the social relevance of our research. Building on repeated appeals for the value of field research over time, our immediate response to the most recent crisis promises greater support and opportunities for publishing field research, and, thus, for encouraging psychologists to engage in "real-world" settings and with socially consequential issues.

WHAT DIFFERENCE CAN ENGAGED RESEARCH (AND RESEARCHERS) MAKE?

The history of our field demonstrates that the valuable application of psychological principles beyond the laboratory is not restricted to field research but can also involve direct, *personal* engagement of researchers with other influential institutions and organizations. Some of our field's greatest social impact has come about through specific contributions within the legal system and in the formulation of organizational and public policy. Within the legal system, social psychologists are frequently called upon to testify as expert witnesses, and psychological organizations have provided important amicus briefs in landmark U.S. Supreme Court cases. This personal engagement with social issues and policies is for many psychologists an important way of achieving the goal of applying scholarly knowledge for the benefit of society.

Psychological research evidence has played an influential role in a series of landmark decisions by the U.S. Supreme Court involving discrimination and diversity over the past 60 years. This topic represents only a limited glimpse of the ways psychologists engage with the legal system; other examples include the accuracy of eyewitness testimony (Loftus, 2011), lie detection (e.g., Forrest & Feldman, 2000), ways to reduce excessive force by police (e.g., Center for Policing Equity: http://www.policingequity.org), as well as other topics, such as the effects of pornography and violent video games on behavior. In addition, psychologists work closely with a range of advocacy groups, nonprofit organizations, and educational and financial policymakers.

A brief review of Supreme Court cases illustrates the important role that psychologists can play in shaping law and policy. One of the earliest and most important cases, historically, was *Brown v. Board of Education of Topeka* (1954), which made racial segregation illegal in education. The Society for the Psychological Study of Social Issues offered an influential amicus brief, and the research of Clark and Clark (1947) showing that Black children preferred to play with White rather than Black dolls (indicating a devaluing of their racial group) was formally cited in the court's decision. More recently, the American Psychological Association filed an amicus brief in support of affirmative action policies in the University of Michigan cases reviewed by the Supreme Court (*Gratz v. Bollinger*, 2003; *Grutter v. Bollinger*, 2003). This amicus brief discussed, among other psychological evidence, how Whites have racial biases that they are not fully aware of that can systematically influence how they perceive and respond to Blacks, how Blacks may become sensitive to and preoccupied with cultural stereotypes of their group in ways that adversely influence their academic performance, and how diversity can promote creative problem solving and develop cross-cultural communication skills. In the most recent challenge to the legality of affirmative action heard by the Supreme Court, *Fisher v. University of Texas* (2013), teams of psychologists working with organizations such as the American Psychological Association prepared new amicus briefs.[1]

Psychologists' testimony was also a key factor in a landmark Supreme Court case on gender discrimination (Fiske, Bersoff, Borgida, Deaux, & Heilman, 1991; see also Chapter 6, this volume): *Hopkins v. Price Waterhouse* (1990). Ann Hopkins, the plaintiff, had an outstanding record of

---

[1] See http://www.apa.org/about/offices/ogc/amicus/fisher.pdf for an example of the latest psychological research in an amicus curiae brief to the courts about the benefits of diversity.

accomplishment at the accounting firm of Price Waterhouse, but she was denied promotion to partner. Although Price Waterhouse contended that the reason she was not promoted related to interpersonal skill problems, Hopkins argued that she was denied partnership because of her gender. The American Psychological Association's amicus brief in this case emphasized the role of gender stereotyping. Testimony in the case frequently alluded to the fact that Hopkins did not conform to the traditional feminine stereotype. Fiske et al. (1991) reported,

> According to some evaluators, this "lady partner candidate" was "macho," she "overcompensated for being a woman," and she needed a "course at charm school." A sympathetic colleague advised that she would improve her chances if she would "walk more femininely, talk more femininely, dress more femininely, have her hair styled, and wear jewelry" (*Hopkins v. Price Waterhouse*, 1985, p. 1117). (p. 1050)

The testimony about the nature of gender biases in this case drew directly on psychological research demonstrating that stereotypes operate most strongly to bias perceptions, and in the end penalize people who deviate from these stereotypes when evaluative criteria are ambiguous. Judge Gesell, who presided over the case, ultimately ruled in favor of Hopkins. He concluded that an "employer that treats [a] woman with [an] assertive personality in a different manner than if she had been a man is guilty of sex discrimination" (*Hopkins v. Price Waterhouse*, 1985, p. 1119). Moreover, based on the testimony of psychologists, he acknowledged that "a far more subtle process" than the usual discriminatory intent was operating (p. 1118).

In addition to demonstrating the direct impact that psychology can have in the courtroom through expert testimony, this case illustrates how basic research can sensitize psychologists—and eventually the legal system and the general public—to recognize that subtle social biases exist and can systematically affect decision making. It should be noted that, although psychologists have often been socially and politically engaged to promote liberal policies, some also choose to actively support politically conservative positions (Duarte et al., 2015). Regardless of the political stance researchers take, the goal of this form of engagement by psychologists is to communicate findings of basic research more broadly to avert injustices.

HOW CAN ENGAGEMENT MAKE OUR RESEARCH BETTER?

The intrinsic value of engagement is not limited to promoting the public good. As noted earlier, Lewin encouraged field research and engagement in social issues not only for testing and applying psychological theory but also because these activities can stimulate new theoretical insights. In particular, I wish to highlight two important ways that the broader engagement of psychologists can stimulate and enhance psychological science and promote researchers' professional goals.

Engagement Helps Us to Identify New Research Questions

As scientists, we invest in the process of cumulative knowledge building: Citing empirical precedent is a central element for developing the rationale behind our predictions. While this process is essential for building a valid body of evidence, it limits the likelihood of exploring novel research directions. But there is value in both *continuous discovery*—in which we follow programmatic lines of research—and *discontinuous discovery*—in which we seek out and recognize patterns that do not follow in a logical way from previous work. Researchers' informal and formal engagement outside the confines of the laboratory can thus complement more conventional research approaches to produce a more vibrant science.

One specific illustration of how researchers' informal engagement in applied settings can generate new insights involves the work of Dr. Robert Cialdini. Cialdini developed a reputation as an outstanding theoretician and researcher studying the ways that people influence and persuade others to do things they normally would not do. He credits many of his ideas, though, to the time he invested going "undercover," working in a variety of occupations (e.g., in sales positions of various types, as a waiter) in which persuasion and social influence are critical to success. He talked with, listened to, and learned from people who excelled in these professions—people who knew what techniques and strategies to employ but who did not necessarily know or care about why they worked psychologically. For instance, while he received training to sell cars, Cialdini learned of a technique, lowballing, in which the customer was given a price well below the amount at which the salesperson intended to sell the car, in order to get the customer to commit to the purchase. Then, the offer was either rescinded, ostensibly because the sales manager voided it because the dealership would "lose money on it," or because a "calculation error" was made and certain options were not included in the original price. Once customers committed to buying the car, they were more willing to accept the "sales manager's" higher price or pay more for the car with the "options" calculated into the new price. Cialdini subsequently studied the phenomenon of lowballing in the laboratory, replicating the effect and illuminating the underlying processes of the psychology of commitment. He wrote scholarly articles and books for both the profession and the public to communicate his findings broadly to help people understand and resist manipulation (see Cialdini, 2009a).

While the profession is generally comfortable with the process of moving from the laboratory to the field, the idea of having an applied problem stimulate and shape psychological research and theory is less commonly valued in the profession. Nevertheless, more formal research endeavors in field settings also have the potential to inject new perspectives into a particular researcher's program of inquiry, as well as in social psychological science more generally. Paluck and Cialdini (2014) offered concrete advice about how to conduct field research while highlighting its value for new theory development in at least three ways: (a) by helping researchers define and refine their theoretical constructs in order to apply them in a naturalistic setting, (b) by assessing a theory's pragmatic worth, and (c) by making social psychological research relevant to a broad audience.

Engagement Can Transform the Scope of What We Study

In contrast to the steady and often slow accumulation of scientific knowledge from the laboratory, the real world presents a series of crises that require immediate attention. While most scholars accept the adage that "necessity is the mother of invention," the role of such necessity is often underappreciated in terms of its contributions to contemporary psychological science. However, engaging in efforts to address timely social problems has valuable scholarly, disciplinary, and societal benefits by changing the scope of the issues we study.

Take, for example, AIDS (see Fisher, Fisher, & Shuper, 2014). This issue attracted considerable attention in medicine, immunology, epidemiology, and, to a more limited degree, psychology. Relevant theory already existed at the time, but its application to the immediate crisis was not obvious, and extant theory was insufficient to fully address the kinds of issues (e.g., social stigma) involved in preventing the spread of AIDS. Addressing the AIDS epidemic thus stimulated rapid theory development as well as the creation of practical interventions to reduce risky sexual practices. The information–motivation–behavioral skills model (Fisher et al., 2014), for example, explained how information can be directed toward specific aspects of attitudes, and emphasized how reinforcing or creating appropriate motivation and teaching relevant behavioral skills can further influence behavioral intentions and, ultimately, health-promoting behavior.

The impact of psychological work on AIDS prevention has had a significant social impact. Despite the medical community's confidence that it could cure AIDS in a limited time with sufficient resources, there is still no cure for the disease. Psychologists did, however, make significant strides in reducing the spread of AIDS through theory-based interventions. This work is particularly important for two reasons. First, because more people with AIDS are living longer and having more active lives, adopting behaviors that prevent the spread the virus to others is even more important. Second, recent medical advances in this area require people living with AIDS to faithfully manage their treatment, and psychological interventions have greatly improved adherence. Moreover, to the extent that people with serious but common health conditions, such as diabetes and obesity, benefit significantly from behavioral management, the theory, research, and interventions stimulated by psychologists' responses to the AIDS epidemic have even broader applicability.

CONCLUSION

Engagement in social issues is assumed by some to be antithetical to rigorous scholarship. Nevertheless, engagement in applied issues and topics of public debate in appropriate measure can enhance the quality and creativity of one's own scholarly work. It can do so by reinforcing the motivation that initially attracted so many of us to the field. As Paluck and Cialdini (2014) observed,

> Most students in social psychology are drawn to the discipline because of an interest in the world around them, but in the course of study, their eyes are retrained to find inspiration in abstract theory and to observe and test these theoretical processes in laboratories. (p. 82)

For many of us, in the absence of seeing how our research matters, our motivations for doing the work can easily wane. Intrinsic motivation to pursue research questions is essential for a successful academic career.

Indeed, my own engagement experiences—ranging from consulting with the Department of Defense about how to promote the advancement of members of racial and ethnic minority groups in the military to serving as a member of an Institute of Medicine panel on racial disparities in health care—redirected the trajectory of my career. These experiences provided new lenses for me to use to understand bias, created new research opportunities, and challenged me to consider structural- and institutional-level influences, as well as the interpersonal and intergroup forces with which I was familiar and comfortable. To put it simply, engagement outside the lab made me a better scholar.

Engagement beyond the confines of the research laboratory is also important for our discipline. Field research that tests psychological theory in applied settings can help ensure the replicability of an effect and identify new boundary conditions. Through personal engagement in social issues, psychologists can directly promote public welfare and enhance the standing of the field both in scientific circles and among policymakers and general audiences. Through engagement, psychologists can also discover new questions, perspectives, and results that shape theory development in creative ways.

People often think about the apparent tension between engagement and research, and they feel that they must choose one or the other. In principle, though, these activities can and should be complementary rather than oppositional. In practice, in which time and resources are limited, there are indeed trade-offs. Nevertheless, for those so inclined to pursue both, it can be energizing and generative—two essential components to advancing our scholarship. Understanding how these activities can facilitate each other is, therefore, critical to making one's research matter.

REFERENCES

Brown v. Board of Education of Topeka, 347 U.S. 483 (1954).

Buhrmester, M., Kwang, T., & Gosling, S. D. (2011). Amazon's Mechanical Turk: A new source of inexpensive, yet high-quality, data? *Perspectives on Psychological Science, 6*, 3–5. http://dx.doi.org/10.1177/1745691610393980

Cialdini, R. B. (1980). Full-circle social psychology. In L. Bickman (Ed.), *Applied social psychology annual* (Vol. 1, pp. 21–47). Beverly Hills, CA: Sage.

Cialdini, R. B. (2009a). *Influence: Science and practice* (5th ed.). Boston, MA: Allyn & Bacon.

Cialdini, R. B. (2009b). We have to break up. *Perspectives on Psychological Science, 4*, 5–6. http://dx.doi.org/10.1111/j.1745-6924.2009.01091.x

Clark, K. B., & Clark, M. P. (1947). Racial identification and preference in Negro children. In T. M. Newcomb & E. L. Hartley (Eds.), *Readings in social psychology* (pp. 602–611). New York, NY: Holt.

Dovidio, J. F. (2001, Winter). On the nature of contemporary prejudice: The third wave. *Journal of Social Issues, 57*, 829–849. http://dx.doi.org/10.1111/0022-4537.00244

Dovidio, J. F., Gaertner, S. L., & Pearson, A. R. (2017). Aversive racism and contemporary bias. In F. K. Barlow & C. G. Sibley (Eds.), *The Cambridge handbook of the psychology of prejudice* (pp. 267–294). Cambridge, England: Cambridge University Press.

Duarte, J. L., Crawford, J. T., Stern, C., Haidt, J., Jussim, L., & Tetlock, P. E. (2015). Political diversity will improve social psychological science. *Behavioral and Brain Sciences, 38*, e130.

Fisher v. University of Texas, 133 S. Ct. 2411 (2013).

Fisher, W. A., Fisher, J. D., & Shuper, P. A. (2014). Social psychology and the fight against AIDS: An information-motivation-behavioral skills model for the prediction and promotion of health behavior change. *Advances in*

Experimental Social Psychology, 50, 106–192. http://dx.doi.org/10.1016/B978-0-12-800284-1.00003-5

Fiske, S. T., Bersoff, D. N., Borgida, E., Deaux, K., & Heilman, M. E. (1991). Social science research on trial: Use of sex stereotyping research in Price Waterhouse v. Hopkins. *American Psychologist, 46,* 1049–1060. http://dx.doi.org/10.1037/0003-066X.46.10.1049

Forrest, J. A., & Feldman, R. S. (2000). Detecting deception and judge's involvement: Lower task involvement leads to better lie detection. *Personality and Social Psychology Bulletin, 26,* 118–125. http://dx.doi.org/10.1177/0146167200261011

Gergen, K. J. (1973). Social psychology as history. *Journal of Personality and Social Psychology, 26,* 309–320. http://dx.doi.org/10.1037/h0034436

Gratz v. Bollinger, 539 U.S. 244 (2003).

Greenwald, A. G., & Krieger, L. H. (2006). Implicit bias: Scientific foundations. *California Law Review, 94,* 945–967. http://dx.doi.org/10.2307/20439056

Greenwald, A. G., Poehlman, T. A., Uhlmann, E. L., & Banaji, M. R. (2009). Understanding and using the Implicit Association Test: III. Meta-analysis of predictive validity. *Journal of Personality and Social Psychology, 97,* 17–41. http://dx.doi.org/10.1037/a0015575

Grutter v. Bollinger, 539 U.S. 306 (2003).

Hopkins v. Price Waterhouse, 618 F. Supp. 1109 (D.D.C. 1985), *aff'd in part, rev'd in part,* 825 F.2d 458 (D.C. Cir. 1987), *aff'd in part, rev'd in part,* 490 U.S. 228 (1989).

Hopkins v. Price Waterhouse, 737 F. Supp. 1202 (D.D.C. 1990) (on remand).

LaCour, M. J., & Green, D. P. (2014, December). When contact changes minds: An experiment on transmission of support for gay equality [Retracted]. *Science, 346,* 1366–1369. http://dx.doi.org/10.1126/science.1256151

Lammers, J., & Stapel, D. A. (2011). Racist biases in legal decisions are reduced by a justice focus [Retracted]. *European Journal of Social Psychology, 41,* 375–387.

Lewin, K. (1946). Action research and minority problems. *Journal of Social Issues, 2,* 34–46. http://dx.doi.org/10.1111/j.1540-4560.1946.tb02295.x

Loftus, E. F. (2011). How I got started: From semantic memory to expert testimony. *Applied Cognitive Psychology, 25,* 347–348. http://dx.doi.org/10.1002/acp.1769

Maner, J. K. (2016). Into the wild: Field research can increase both replicability and real-world impact. *Journal of Experimental Social Psychology, 66,* 100–106. http://dx.doi.org/10.1016/j.jesp.2015.09.018

Open Science Collaboration. (2015). Estimating the reproducibility of psychological science. *Science, 349,* 943. http://dx.doi.org/10.1126/science.aac4716

Paluck, E. L., & Cialdini, R. B. (2014). Field research methods. In H. T. Reis & C. M. Judd (Eds.), *Handbook of research methods in social and personality psychology* (2nd ed., pp. 81–98). New York, NY: Oxford University Press.

Pettigrew, T. F. (1988). Influencing policy with social psychology. *Journal of Social Issues, 44,* 205–219. http://dx.doi.org/10.1111/j.1540-4560.1988.tb02071.x

Rodin, J. (1985). The application of social psychology. In G. Lindzey & E. Aronson (Eds.), *The handbook of social psychology* (3rd ed., Vol. 2, pp. 805–881). New York, NY: Random House.

Ruys, K. I., & Stapel, D. A. (2008). The secret life of emotions. *Psychological Science, 19,* 385–391. http://dx.doi.org/10.1111/j.1467-9280.2008.02097.x

Simmons, J. P., Nelson, L. D., & Simonsohn, U. (2011). False-positive psychology: Undisclosed flexibility in data collection and analysis allows presenting anything as significant. *Psychological Science, 22,* 1359–1366. http://dx.doi.org/10.1177/0956797611417632

Index

About the Editor

Linda R. Tropp, PhD, is a professor of social psychology at the University of Massachusetts Amherst, from which she received the Distinguished Academic Outreach Award for excellence in the application of scientific knowledge to advance the public good. A Fellow of the American Psychological Association and the Society of Experimental Social Psychology, Tropp has received scholarly awards from the Society for the Psychological Study of Social Issues and the International Society of Political Psychology. She has been cited in numerous news outlets (including *New York Times, Boston Globe, Wall Street Journal, New Republic, O Magazine, U.S. News and World Report, Salon,* and *Huffington Post,* among others), invited to author blogs for *Psychology Today* and the *American Psychological Association,* and interviewed on radio and television (including *PBS News Hour, NPR's Talk of the Nation,* and *New England Public Radio*). She has presented social science research at several Congressional briefings and has worked with national organizations to translate research evidence for U.S. Supreme Court cases relevant to racial integration, discrimination, and immigration. She regularly works on state and national initiatives to improve interracial relations and promote racial justice, and with international organizations to evaluate programs designed to reduce racial and ethnic conflict. Tropp is coeditor of *Moving Beyond Prejudice Reduction: Pathways to Positive Intergroup Relations* (2011), coauthor of *When Groups Meet: The Dynamics of Intergroup Contact* (2011), and editor of *The Oxford Handbook of Intergroup Conflict* (2012).